Yi Jing Ethics

YI JING ETHICS

LESSONS OF A DAOIST MASTER FROM THE WUDANG MOUNTAINS

BY XING DE
TRANSLATED BY JOHAN HAUSEN

purple cloud
press

Hardcover ISBN-13: 978-1-991081-04-9
Softcover ISBN-13: 978-1-991081-03-2

FRONT COVER ART
Spirit Turtle Illustration (shengui tu 神龜圖) by the Jin Dynasty painter
Zhang Gui 張珪 (active 1156–1161)

PHOTOGRAPHY LI SHIFU
Chrisina Chandler

COVER DESIGN
Anne-Maree Taranto

INTERIOR DESIGN
Barbara Tada

Published by Purple Cloud Press:
purplecouldinstitute.com
purplecloudpress@gmail.com

To the nine sages who created the Yi Jing:
Fu Xi, the Divine Farmer, the Yellow Emperor,
Emperor Yao, Emperor Shun, Yu, the Great, King Wen,
the Duke of Zhou and Confucius, and of course,
my teacher, Li Shifu, who opened this sacred book for me

PURPLE CLOUD'S VISION

PURPLE CLOUD PRESS was founded on the principle that only by merging theoretical knowledge and practical experience is one able to gain true understanding and grasp the nuances of pertinent writings. Therefore, all publications by Purple Cloud Press are underpinned by this principle of scholar-physicians and scholar-practitioners into the following threefold mission:

- To publish the works of the founders of the Purple Cloud Institute and other author's finished works in the field of medicine, Asian religions and martial arts,
- To translate original ancient Asian texts into the English language,
- To commission writings about masters' and teachers' lineage traditions.

Purple Cloud Press incentivizes authors and translators by letting them retain a large percentage of the royalties to encourage continued translation projects as well as by providing a platform to reach the largest possible readership. Purple Cloud Press strongly believes that this will help make accessible the profundity of treasures previously hidden from the English-speaking world.

purple cloud
press

近又讀易，見一意思：聖人作易，本是使人卜筮，以決所行之可否，而因之以教人為善。

When I [, Zhu Xi,] recently once more read the *Yi [Jing]*, I saw one of its meanings. When the sages created the *Yi [Jing]*, it was originally intended to enable people to divine through turtle shells and milfoil, in order to determine what could be conducted and what not. By doing so, they taught people to act out the good.

—晦庵先生朱文公文集·答張敬夫
Literary Collection from Teacher Hui'an,
Zhu the Illustrious Elder; 'Reply to Zhang Jingfu'

Contents

興德

XING DE (LI SHIFU)

Li Shifu performing a high priest ceremony[1]

俗名 ;杜松峰，道名 ;兴德（别名 ;理丰、诚道、宗常、大家都称他理师傅）1964 年出生在河南省商丘，从 12 岁就开始先后学习外家少林功夫，内家武当太极功夫和佛教、天主教、基督教、伊斯兰教经典，他去了中

国的很多的大山寻找高人老师，拜了很多师傅所以他
有很多名字。1991年起他正式成为一个道教信徒，1996
年他离开家在武当山成为一个正式出家人，并在湖北
省十堰市张湾区白马山找到了他自己的路，在艰苦的
状况下经历了许多磨难，跟随他的师傅继续习修炼内
丹、学习传统道医、道教符法、咒语等道术。自2000
年起他成为五仙庙的住持，是三十代武当山龙门派和
高功经忏法师。现任张湾区道协会长。师傅说；不要
宣传我，我就是一个要饭人，能活着就已经非常感谢
上帝了，名利荣辱已经看淡了，全世界70亿人能够有
缘相见的能有几个，是天大的因缘，你们能够把所教
的内容学好，用好，能够帮助别人，我就很高兴了。

LI SHIFU'S (1964–) common name is Du Songfeng and his Daoist name is Xing De or Flourishing Virtue. His other names are Li Feng, Cheng Dao and Zong Chang, but everyone calls him Li Shifu. He was born in 1964 in Shangqiu city, Henan Province, China. At the age of twelve, Xing De began to study the external martial arts of Shaolin and the internal martial arts of Wudang *taiji gongfu*, as well as the classical scriptures of Buddhism, Christianity and Islam. He travelled to many high mountains in China in order to seek out grandmasters. He was accepted as a disciple by many of these masters and has therefore received many names.

In 1991, Xing De officially became a devotee and follower of the *dao*. In 1996, he left his home and formally became a renunciant in Wudang, and later found his own path at White Horse Mountain in Shiyan city, Zhangwang District, Hubei Province, where he experienced a great deal of suffering and hardship in very harsh conditions. He learned cultivation practices in internal alchemy from his master and received the transmissions of Daoist Medicine and Daoist talismans, rituals, incantations and other Daoist arts. In 2000, he became the abbot of the Five Immortals Temple. Li Shifu is a 30th-generation high priest of the Wudang Dragon Gate Sect and is also a master of Scriptural Repentance ceremonies:

> I don't want to advertise myself, as I'm only
> a beggar. Being alive I'm already very grateful to
> the deities. I look indifferently at fame, wealth,
> honour and glory. Of the seven billion people in the
> entire world, how many of them are you destined
> to meet? This certainly must be a predestined
> relationship as vast as the heavens. If students
> learn the transmitted content well, apply it well,
> and are capable of helping other people, I'm already
> completely happy.
>
> —Li Shifu

INTRODUCTION

BY LI SHIFU

I N ANCIENT CHINA the *Yi Jing*[2] was the first of all the scriptures to appear. It is ranked higher than the *Zhuang Zi*[3] and even higher than the *Daode Jing*, as well as the Four Books[4] and Five Classics[5] of Confucianism. This is how important a position it holds. The binary code used by modern computers is derived from the *Yi Jing*.[6] So the east and west have taken this in surprisingly different directions. In the west the binary notion was developed on the material level to manufacture computers, while in China it evolved on a philosophical and spiritual level. But the *Yi Jing* is several thousand years old.

In the title of the *Yi Jing*, the two radicals of the sun 日 and moon 月 combine into the character for 'Changes' 易.[7] The most ancient Chinese character for 'sun' was a circle with a black dot inside it, while the moon at that time was depicted as a crescent. The character for 'change' thus reflects the transformation of the sun and moon in their cycle from nothingness to existence and back again, and in this way it represents the great *dao*. It is

like the process of growth when *yin* and *yang* harmoniously form
an embryo from the egg or ovum and sperm. One moon passes
after another until ten moons have passed and there is a newborn
baby, which then progresses from youth to middle age, old age
and death – this is the wheel of nature. The circuit of the sun and
moon is the same from morning to evening.[8] The life and death
of the ten thousand things on earth follows the same cycle:

日月為易。

The [characters of the] sun and moon become [the
character] 'changes'.[9]

The *Yi Jing* is very mysterious. No one knows where it came from.
But it has been passed down all the way from ancient times until
now. Two thousand years ago, Qin Shihuang[10] had many books
burned in the Qin Dynasty named after him, but the *Yi Jing* was
not among them. Qin Shihuang was opposed to many books, but
he chose not to incinerate this one, as it did not contradict the
principles of cosmology. So valuable is the *Yi Jing* that even the
Qin Emperor found it indispensable.

The earliest records of the origins of the *Yi Jing* are the Yellow
River Map and the Luo River Scroll,[11] so called because they are
said to have emerged out of rivers. Out of the He River a gigan-
tic turtle bubbled up, which radiated light. It was as though fire
were being spewed out of the water. Does such a great turtle with
light and fire exist? You can imagine for yourself what it might
have been.[12] In the Luo River, a fire-spitting dragon, shape-shift-
ing, powerful and mighty, also came out of the water. The Yellow
River Map and Luo River Scroll, which are the foundation of the
Yi Jing, were then transmitted to earthlings, who at the time were

closer to animals than people.[13] But regardless of the mythological origins of the *Yi Jing*, it is also truly marvellous in its applications.

The *Yi Jing* can answer any question. For elementary school children, it responds at an elementary school level, for middle school pupils, it answers at the middle school level, and for professors it communicates at their own level. It will speak to you on your own respective level. It knows our everyday life and is as relevant for people today as it was several thousand years ago, when work involved farming the land and hunting. The *Yi Jing* knows how to connect with the heavens and earth and with the spirits in the heavens. The hexagrams and their meanings always stay the same, but through our experience with the book and our understanding of it, we make hexagrams dynamic and applicable to any situation. So this is how you should use it. It will work because humans always act, too readily, from the place of their own needs and desires. The *Yi Jing* came to lead us out of that. To understand the *Yi Jing* you need to grasp that its main purpose is to help you to unite with the *dao* and you need to know how to do that.

The *Yi Jing* has innumerable details while its design provides an outline, like the countless hairs on a body. It will give you the means to explore calendrical calculations[14] and everything in it has fixed numbers.[15] The *Yi Jing* oracle is relevant to any situation, whether inside or outside of society. Anything which falls within the principles of *yin* and *yang* can be predicted by the *Yi Jing*. As is stated in *The Scripture of the Hidden Talisman*,[16] to take control of *yin* and *yang* is to control your life, because you know how to transform it. Then you are no longer subject to its natural law. The *Yi Jing* is like searching on the internet – you enter within and whatever you want, you can find. You should know that the *Yi Jing* is employed for casting oracles in many fields, including military strategy and government affairs, but we use it to guide us through our lives. For example, if we are about to attempt something, we can ask the *Yi Jing*: 'Will I succeed in this task? Will it help me in my life? Will it help others? What will be the outcome?' If we enter a competition, we can ask: 'Will I win or will I lose?' It can also tell you step by step how an outcome will be achieved. If you are looking for a new job, you can ask: 'How will this turn out? Will it work out for me?' Or if someone is ill, you can ask the *Yi Jing*: 'What kind of sickness does this person have? Where did they get it?' So the book encompasses all events. Everything is included.

Some of you have already studied the *Yi Jing* before coming to China, along with *fengshui* and so forth. But how much did you really understand? I have taught not even one tenth of it in the past. The quantity of information that it contains is just too great. If you can study only one or two tenths of the *Yi Jing* and use it purposefully, that is already quite good. But who is really able to use the Six Lines Method[17] of the *Yi Jing*? Compared to the meanings of the Tarot cards, the *Yi Jing* is much deeper and more detailed in content. You need to spend a lot of time in study before you can enter its portals. You must study well the Six Lines Method alone – do not study anything else – because you all live in the city, where you can use it. Many decisions on matters such as timing, work, and general affairs require the *Yi Jing*'s judgement. As soon as you have the book, you have your tool. Then it should be easy for you to employ the method to find whatever you need. There are a great many methods for healing. We are going to study just one, and a rather old one: healing by means of the *Yi Jing*. Ten to fifteen percent of *Yi Jing* methods are about predicting and resolving ailments. When healing through the *Yi Jing*, there is no need to prescribe medicine.

As a healer you tell the patient how to make crucial adjustments to their life. There are innumerable such methods of healing. With regard to those of the *Yi Jing*, if each person were to pay you one Fen[18] for a reading, you could earn a living from that. Such an occupation would probably be a lot healthier in lifestyle than a normal job, such as office work. But you need money to live in society, so if you do not work then somebody has to buy you rice and flour. For an itinerant priest or a wandering monk, if you arrive somewhere and have no food, then if you know the *Yi Jing* you can say: 'I will cast an oracle for you, and you can give me as much as you please in return.' If that person is rich, they can give more. It does not matter. Thus, you will be guaranteed to survive on the road. This is not something you do to accumulate or hoard money. Having food to eat is enough, or to buy a plane ticket if you need one, and then you are off:

四海為家 。
The four seas are my home.

I have already lived here on White Horse Mountain for twenty years. I want to run away but I cannot.[19] By making an effort in society, you will receive a reasonable amount of money in recompense, but you must be able to balance this with frugality and not succumb to greed. Many great masters who study life have provided hexagram calculations[20] for CEOs and other bosses only, not for commoners. Would they be successful in their great business undertakings? Important issues have to be resolved, to the tune of one or two hundred thousand Yuan. The CEOs want to excel in their business and say to the master: 'I will give you ten per cent of the profits if it is successful!' Pay attention to how this is done. Because you can find the problem through the *Yi Jing*, you can then solve it and help the plan to succeed. But this is not our purpose here, which is healing. Nevertheless, to provide healing treatments in society is first to make a reasonable living. We do not do this out of greed as that would only be to increase our desires. On the contrary, we calculate hexagrams and thereby treatments for cancer patients, for example, and thereby save their lives. You might say: 'I am giving you your life back. How much is that worth? I am selling you your life.' And they would reply: 'I do not care about money, I just want to keep my life.' There is no point in having a great deal of money when you have no life in which to use it. They have finally grasped the importance of life. Even so, there are some people who even at the point of death will still be thinking about how to take their money with them. People in society have to use external instruments and methods, since they have not opened up the internal tools that arise from spiritual practice. If you have such internal means, then why would you still calculate?[21]

I like to tell stories and jokes, but they all share certain principles. I will reprimand you if, based on your interpretation of the six lines, you are looking for our temple dog here, Hua Dou,[22] in India as it were – in other words, if the orientation or direction of your thinking is wrong. This includes the heavenly order, its principles and timeliness, and the earthly principles or geography, human affairs, and common conventions. If you contravene them and go against common practices, you do not combine with life and become one with it. The one per cent of people who are beyond these common situations cannot be judged easily through divinations and you cannot control them. Everyone else might be eating lunch, but they have been fasting for days. They are beyond ordinary considerations and this does not apply to them.[23]

When using the *Yi Jing*, you should ask just one question.

專心一意。
Your mind should be focused, with a single intent.

Moreover, just as in the past, one rule is that you must never draw more than two or three hexagrams for a single issue. Just one is best. Secondly, you must be in a certain frame of mind. Sometimes, if you're very clear in your method of communication,[24] you might calculate a hexagram and the event that you forecast turns out to be the right one and then a couple of months later you return to your notes and realise that you calculated wrongly.[25] The fourth and fifth dimensions are full of mischievous spirits. In time you'll begin to understand what this means.[26]

I began to research the *dao* in 1985, more than thirty years ago, which is why I know the difference between the straight path of Daoism and the heterodox side paths. Thus, I know how the *Yi Jing* can easily lead a student of the *dao* in a wrong direction.[27]

The *Yi Jing* is cosmologically based on the changes of the heavenly *qi* and its movements, as well as *yin* and *yang*, the five phases, the heavenly stems and the twelve earthly branches, which all form its foundation. It would take too long to teach every aspect of *Yi Jing* divination, so we will have to take some shortcuts. Cheng Tong, one of my senior students, studied the Six Lines Method for three to four hours each day. In total, he studied for more than five months, just so he could understand this one aspect only: healing. He did well in that method, though even five whole months did not give him time enough to study other basic methods such as the four pillars and the eight characters.[28] You must study how to find out the illnesses of people through the *Yi Jing* as its highest goal. You do so by using the five phases – wood, fire, earth, metal and water – along with the ten heavenly stems and the twelve earthly branches, and also *yin* and *yang* and their mutual unification.[29]

Casting oracles for illness is only one aspect of the *Yi Jing*. There are other domains such as travel, weddings, and commerce. In total, there are twenty-two or so aspects, including construction projects and employment. We will explore just one aspect. In Daoist Medicine we study the influence of *fengshui* on the body. We focus on its methods to address health problems. Likewise, that is all that is involved in using the *Yi Jing* to treat illness. The protest and revolt of the body has no language in which it can express itself. If your heart jumped out and started talking, you would run away in fear, yet many people know well what is wrong with them but ignore it. So, when you encounter health problems, use this method. It is very fast working and will resolve issues in just one or two days.

You must learn how to use the *Yi Jing* as it is a great tool. It can be likened to a key that opens the door of a car. If you wish to enter into the *Yi Jing* more deeply, you must study all sixty-four hexagrams and for this you need to have a very capacious memory. The numbers[30] of pre-heaven and post-heaven arrangements, the five phases, the supporting and controlling cycles, and the transforming, insulting and unification cycles[31] are all related to human life.

Without this foundation it is impossible to study the *Yi Jing* successfully. We must begin with *yin* and *yang*, the five phases, the eight trigrams,[32] the Yellow River Map, the Luo River Scroll and learn how to consult the lunar calendar. The west uses the Gregorian calendar,[33] yet what we are looking for does not exist within it, such as the Twenty-Eight Constellations, the heavenly stems and earthly branches and the black and yellow paths, as well as other auspicious and inauspicious dates of the lunar calendar.[34] You would need very good brain functions, were you to convert the time between the east and west manually.[35] We need to study all of this and more. The topics are all interlinked and integrated together. Such a vast study is just too much to talk about fully, so I wish to draw this to a close. But what you must study if you enter deeply into the *Yi Jing* includes *yin* and *yang*, the calendrical calculations of the Four Pillars, the Six Lines Method, the Plum Blossom Art[36] and the Iron Plate Spirit Book.[37]

With regard to divination, sometimes in the morning a group of city people will come up to the mountain and want me to foretell the future. These are the needs of city people: 'you want a safe and sound family? I can help you. You have disaster and misfortune at home? No problem, I can help you. But you want to start a business and get rich? You want to become the Deity of Wealth? You want to become an official? I am not Xi Jinping[38] – this is a headache.'

After many decades of study with many teachers, as the *Yi Jing* is closely interwoven with longevity and life, I finally decided to teach it. I have seen many students become specialists in the *Yi Jing* for economic reasons. This practice violates our purpose, so I made up my mind to stop teaching it, hence this may be the last time I do so. It is not easy to follow this course. You might have to draw on all of your brain cells for the memorizations it requires. We are not a school, but there are studies. We are not a hospital, but there are regulations. We are in a religious space, but there are no strict requirements.

For weddings, receiving guests, childbirth, travel, building houses, and marriage, all Chinese fortune-tellers predict good fortune. Do they not get tired of living this way? Even for the birth of a child they must find a suitable date! Is childbirth not a natural occurrence? They say: 'This is a bad time to give birth! This is a good time!' In the past there was no Caesarean surgery or inductions, hence it was not possible to fix a date for childbirth, but nowadays they can shift it even ten days forward. If, as with these fortune-tellers, your way of thinking is problematic and you study the *Yi Jing*, then you will deviate from the central purpose of the *Yi Jing* for us, namely healing, as well as from the goal of our teachings. Likewise, *gongfu*[39] is not only for fighting or sparring. We must also have *gongfu* compassion.[40] Just as the study of Daoist medicine[41] imparts skills that enable us to help others and to relieve their suffering, so too does studying the *Yi Jing*, whose purpose becomes corrupted if this is not our aim. Why do I teach the *Yi Jing*? Because it enables you to find out what influences the health and wellbeing of the human body:

醫道同 。

Medicine and the *dao* are one and the same.

Any disease that cannot be detected through tests and computers in hospitals, you can discover through your knowledge of the *Yi Jing*. Once you have found the problem, you can then solve it. The same applies to *fengshui*,[42] as it also affects our health and body and creates illnesses.[43] The goal of the study is to find out where there is good *fengshui*.[44] If you approach the *Yi Jing* saying, 'I want to get rich!', this is not in accordance with my teachings. If you ask, 'How can I obtain great authority and an official position?', this is also not the way that we are following. Our aim is to study and remove that which negatively influences our body in the field of time and space. The following saying is also true of the *Yi Jing*: 'Life comes first, not money or status.' The aim of the *Yi Jing* as a cultivation tool is to harmonize people with the universe and to unify them with the heavens and earth in order to better understand the world, life, people and nature. This enables them to relieve their suffering and cure their present and future diseases. However, those very high masters or sages who have already grasped hold of their life[45] are no longer predictable by the natural laws on which the prognostications of the *Yi Jing* are based, as they have gone beyond them.

There are many ways to study the *Yi Jing* and many roads you can follow. Some people learn a subject and then put it down. It is like yeast in cold weather, when it does not ferment. Maybe ten or twenty years later you will ferment, when the weather is warmer. You read a book when you are younger and it holds no meaning for you at that moment. When you are older, you read it again and there is a new knowledge in it which you can then grasp:

> 學習認知實踐總結。
> Study, recognize [the meaning of what you are
> studying], put [that knowledge] into practice, and
> [be able] to sum up [the essence of it].

This is human life. Maybe years later you will be able to distil the essence of the teachings of the *Yi Jing*, and after this will come the transformation of your mind. Some things cannot be brought with you on that path:[46]

> 一分錢帶不走。
> You cannot take even a dime with you.

Why does our *Yi Jing* course include the practice of *gong*[47] and sitting meditation as a requirement? We have to transcend the *Yi Jing* in order to look back at it with true understanding. Thus, the *Yi Jing* has eight Chinese characters that sum up its purpose and it has been said that these might be meditation practices:

寂然不動感而遂通。

Quiet and unmoving, perceive it and succeed in
communion.[48]

These are the most important characters in the *Yi Jing*. The first
two, *jiran* 寂然, mean 'still and stopping', which refers to the
cessation of all electrical impulses and discharges in the brain.
The second two characters, *budong* 不動, also mean 'stopping' or
'unmoving', in both a physical and mental sense. If you move in a
disordered and chaotic way, how can you become still? This stillness is the true meaning of the *Yi Jing* and it comes from sitting
meditation. A common person may try to use the *Yi Jing* to tell
fortunes, cast oracles and predict the future, but they cannot open
up its deeper meanings. The fifth character, *gan* 感, means 'to feel',
'to sense' and 'to perceive' – not only with the sixth sense, but even
with the seventh sense![49] Which brings us to the last three characters, *er suitong* 而遂通 which describe the opening of your third
eye to commune from this third dimension to higher dimensions.
This is why you need to find absolute serenity.

There are three conditions if one wishes to commune between
dimensions. Firstly, this requires sound, voices, and music, such
as that employed in musical healing.[50] Secondly, it requires
incense.[51] In the past you also had to have an altar. You had to
pray and to light incense. There were three platforms with steps
between them[52] and the altar was kept very clean. This was the
designated place for lighting incense, praying and ceremonies: a place for communicating between heaven and earth. In
Catholicism, Buddhism and Daoism alike, the goal of incense is
to commune with heaven and to purify. This communion is why
incense is extremely important. Before playing the zither, you
must wash your hands and the same applies to lighting incense.

The third condition is that of one's thoughts. This can be exemplified in just one word: 'sincerity'.[53] This is the word that is your generation name as my students.[54] Sincerity is the most important thing of all.

一誠通天地。
Single-minded sincerity communes with heaven and earth.[55]

A sincere heart can move up to heaven or down into the earth. Your thoughts must not be fragmented or scattered, but pure and single-minded in honesty and sincerity. When you light incense, perform music or engage in the *Yi Jing*, you must be single-minded in sincerity.

To recapitulate: Whatever your practice, be still and unmoving and maybe a portal will open. This is one example of how to open the gate. In today's language this is called a special ability. You will comprehend what this entails as soon as you see things beyond ordinary perception. You will be able to recognize and become aware of any external energetic field.[56] This is a skill that arises from spiritual practice – you do not need to have an innate ability. Practise sitting meditation persistently and you will just see and feel it.

So now you can understand the eight characters. If you have not acquired such special abilities, you have to use external, material tools and be able to calculate. One plus one equals two, two plus two equals four, and eight times eight equals sixty-four hexagrams. If you have inner tools, special abilities, then you can get rid of the external ones. Start with the *Yi Jing* like building a house from the bottom up, step by step, and in the final stage remove the external structure. As with the scriptures, such as the *Daode Jing*, when you have finally understood them, you can let go of them. Do not rest at the foundation but keep moving up. The *Yi Jing* is a vast subject, no one can become a master of it in just a few days.

The aim of your predictions is crucial. Make health your main focus[57] and priority. Equilibrium is a key principle here. People often consult the *Yi Jing* about possessions, houses, cars and property, but if you are physically suffering every day, this is not a good way to be. If you have no life to use, this is an issue. Everything is built on top of one's quality of life. If you are alive, you need to have good health. Life without health is to suffer in the shadows, to experience stress, pressure and constraints.

It takes several decades to study and research just one aspect of the *Yi Jing*, and each has its own methods. These aspects are all connected and so each must be studied well, and you also need to study the appropriate hand symbols, rituals, incantations, and talismans, in order to purify your thoughts and your space:

沒有練功不行。

To lack the practice of *gong* is not acceptable.

If you do not practise these, then you will not have power, and your castings will all be empty. If you do practise them and thus possess a strong energetic field, *they*[58] will see this very clearly. So you must practise your *gong*. You need to understand the importance of this. All the masters of the past practised *gong*.

As we immerse ourselves in the *Yi Jing* during these lectures, let go of whatever you have studied in the past, regardless of what that might be. Your time here is very short, so drop all past things. Right now you must strive for stillness and purity, and your mind should be located in just one place only: in the eye of your belly.[59] As soon as your thoughts run away with themselves, bring the mind back to that place. But you can spend ten or twenty years attempting to retrieve the mind in this way without fully succeeding. It is a very great task. Yet as long as you can grasp hold of the mind, you can train and tame the tiger and monkey,[60] and eventually the mind will be quiet and still. Do not be scared of any visions you might see in meditation, but also do not follow them out of curiosity. If you comply with this, you will be able to go higher and higher. If you acquire small abilities, do not feel happy about this as there are much greater abilities, yet it all depends on your individual fortune. To be able to come here to study the *Yi Jing* out of all the eight billion people on earth is already a great good fortune!

CHAPTER ONE

THE YI JING VIRTUES AND KARMA

BY LI SHIFU

L ACKING WISDOM, WE spend our days as though our eyes were closed, feeling our way forward like the blind. As we cannot see ahead, we cast oracles and wish to learn from the sages:

聖人無算。

Sages have no [need for] divinations.

We must try to be like the sages, who are not motivated by gain. They let go of such considerations. Where we are going determines where we will be in the future. There is no need to cast oracles to avoid bad things happening, and we should endure what is bad along with the good. Sages do not calculate out of self-interest. Do you think they would refuse to do what is beneficial if there were no personal gain to be derived from it? So why do we cling onto gain? You must ask yourself: who am I? Where am I? How do I exist in this universe? How long have I existed? And what is time itself? You must slowly come to an understanding of the answers to all these questions. I am not a lecturer dealing with theoretical issues here; I am leading my brothers and sisters on a practical path to solving these problems.

In Daoist and Confucian culture, the *Yi Jing* is sometimes misguidedly considered a tool for divining the gains and losses of people. So people use it out of greed for possessions: 'This is all mine, over there is all mine.' City dwellers only want to experience the good. But one should be more elevated in spirit and character than that. Do not seek only what is good for your own self. How much can you really obtain in this lifetime, when you can take nothing with you at the time of death? Selfish desires must cease at higher levels of cultivation, such as that expressed by the eight characters of the *Yi Jing*:

寂然不動感而遂通。
Quiet and unmoving, perceive [the *dao*] and
succeed in communing with it.

The purpose of the *Yi Jing* can be clearly seen in this statement. If you wish to comprehend the higher and deeper knowledge, you must quieten yourself[61] and commune with heaven and earth. But how can you calm yourself down when you are busy with your stocks and shares, your properties, and your parties? The ancient sages of China took extreme measures to achieve this quietude in seclusion. Wang Chongyang dug himself a hole and lived inside it for three years.[62] Bodhidharma, the founder of Chan Buddhism, came from India to China to live in a tiny cave no bigger than two small rooms and triangular in shape, in order to shelter himself from the rain. He cultivated stillness in this cave for nine years.[63] For how many years did Shakyamuni Buddha live in the forest? No one knows for how long Jesus practised cultivation before he departed from this world.[64] Many great teachers have ascended to the heavens and penetrated the earth. Ninety-nine per cent of them reached there through practices of tranquillity. Though there have been exceptions, as some have already been in possession of wisdom at birth:

生而知之是為聖人。

Those who [possess] knowledge at birth are sages.[65]

Every day you cast hexagrams to see if your stocks and shares will go up or down, or whether your business will be successful or not. 'How much money will I get?' This is what you want to know. But in this way, you have lost the true meaning of the *Yi Jing*. Likewise, if you practise the *Yi Jing* all day long for the sake of gaining fame and reputation, that is not in keeping with Daoist or Confucian principles. There is no compassion or kindness in such an approach. As Confucius stated:

己所不欲勿施於人。

Do not impose on others what you yourself do not desire.[66]

Those who seek material gain strive only for external tools and lose the internal tools that they possess deep within. They do not practise in order to cultivate their higher self but are bent solely on profit, which has a negative karmic influence on their health. In Chinese hospitals, for example, if you have no money, they will not admit you and will let you die, because they have nothing to gain from you. Why would they treat you for free? That is their attitude.

Likewise, when misused, the *Yi Jing* can feed into people's desires, though it admonishes you to do everything with an upright heart and to be noble in character. To consult the *Yi Jing* excessively will affect one's karma:[67]

> 君子得之固窮，小人得之輕命。
>
> When noble people obtain [knowledge of the *dao*],
> they are able to remedy what had been lacking.
> When low people learn [about the *dao*], they only
> take lightly their life-destiny.[68]

Low people take life lightly, yet we need a serious moral framework in life, one that seeks the heavenly virtue, the earthly virtue, and the virtue of the great *dao*.[69] Low people are driven only by their cravings: 'I have only one Rolls Royce, I need two, and I need a private jet, and more money and fame.' Almost every Chinese practitioner of the *Yi Jing* and *fengshui* falls prey to greed in this way and they exploit Daoism for their own ends. That is why there are so many low Daoists and why the real cultivators of Daoism or high-level adepts use divination to help other people.

The numbers of the earth and heavens can be divined, since they are fixed and obvious to the initiated.[70] But one cannot predict what one's thoughts will be in the future. Therefore, human thoughts are generally among the least predictable phenomena. Sometimes our thoughts can climb very high or soar to the heavens, while at other times they can fall very low and descend into the earth. So our thinking is a problem. But if our thoughts and intent are correct, there is nothing that we cannot achieve. However, with regard to their frequency you should not cast *Yi Jing* oracles every day, for this will create trouble, as a casting should be regarded as a ritual and something of rare status. Trivial questions might also offend the deities by summoning them for trifling matters, thus showing a lack of reverence for them. The *Yi Jing* should be used for great events and important matters only. In the past, a great *Yi Jing* master would cast no more than two or three oracles a day to earn a living. You should not cast an oracle for each and every trivial situation. The *Yi Jing* is connected to the heavens, which is why it is a very solemn thing and should not be employed too frequently. It is not possible to impart the *Yi Jing* and its practice to someone who pursues their desires with it, even if only in dreams.

Old thinking patterns are deeply ingrained in people and the body is too important to them. You should not indulge in the comforts of the body, and you should not use the *Yi Jing* to this end, though it is true that a physical body is indispensable for cultivation, which is why the three refuges are one's body, one's life and one's mind.[71] Yet in order to take refuge in these, you need to be able to distinguish between real and false phenomena or you may lose the vehicle of the body unknowingly. You may finally understand the meaning of life on your deathbed, but by then it will be too late. You must start again from scratch right now and study the *dao*.

On this path of studying the *dao* and becoming a healer, there is a stage where the *Yi Jing* will no longer be needed as a tool. But whether your healing potential to influence others is at 110 or 220 in voltage power will depend on the level and extent of your self-cultivation. If your ability to heal others is powerful, you will not need to say anything about it, you will just shake hands, 'Nihao, Good Day!', and that's it. The higher powers will have already cleansed and removed the problem. Without the support of these powers, troubles will afflict you and you will not be able to purge yourself of them. The higher self, which we might also call the great self or the pure self, can cleanse them, but this requires also the assistance of the higher powers, to prevent that such ailments and disease contaminate you in the patient's stead. That is why I do not advocate imagining the patient's cancer within you for healing purposes,[72] because you will potentially harm yourself as the cancer may enter your body through this technique. That is not your own fault but that of your teacher, since they taught you the method improperly.[73] You need the proper method in order to heal the patient without becoming ill yourself. One should not practise without a competent teacher, for otherwise:

老實煉功，老實虛空。

Though one is always refining one's *gong*, it will always be in vain.[74]

Act with kind-heartedness, be helpful to others and on the material level, use whatever money you have in the assistance of others. For most people, if they calculate a hexagram concerning an activity and it indicates that they will lose all their wealth, they will then refrain from that action. But this is not our intent in using the *Yi Jing*. You should let go of that money, even if you know beforehand through a *Yi Jing* reading that you will lose it, and learn from this experience as an example of enduring what is bad without any bias. We must act from compassion and kind-heartedness, and through affection and love, and even if we will lose out thereby, we should still do it regardless. Why then should you cast oracles about the good or bad that might happen to you?[75] Just perform good actions, no matter how much you lose out in consequence. What you are losing is actually your karmic afflictions.[76] So one aspect of casting oracles is your ancestral karma[77] and its afflictions, as you gradually decrease the chains of karma through the enactment of merits. Do not take moral responsibility for what is revealed by the castings.[78] This is very important:

平時修橋鋪路。善事過關買路的錢。
Repair bridges and mend roads everyday.
Meritorious deeds are the toll money [that enables you] to pass the barriers.

Meritorious deeds, just like the *Yi Jing*, can be valuable if applied in assistance to others, like money in a savings account that you can use to cancel out your karmic debts. This is the method for removing evil forces that have accumulated from past wrongdoing. 'I have already done many good things in the past', you might say. But you do not know how many karmic afflictions you are carrying, including those inherited from your immediate ancestors. You do not know how many debts you have incurred and how much money you owe. Every day you are paying back the debts of your parents and grandparents for them:

業障不過三代。
Karmic afflictions are not passed on for more than three generations.

Once you have paid it all back, you can start to save up. Before then, all the money you have will immediately be given to others. But if you have savings, you can buy a house. If you fall ill, you can go to hospital. I am using images from society as examples and metaphors. Such is the power and energy of meritorious deeds at the internal level.

As I have said, if you have performed many meritorious deeds and have helped many people, you may ask yourself, 'how is it that I am unwell?' But there is another level to this matter, namely the spiritual tests that people are given by higher powers. If they test you in this way, you are lucky, for they are looking after you like a child, protecting and taking care of you, and scolding you if you go wrong. This is a great good fortune. Without their reprimands, by casting oracles for selfish reasons you will lose your orientation and will fall into a pit from which you cannot crawl out. If you have understood the consequences of your actions, you can regulate the effects by attending to the causes. By interfering with cause and effect, you can thus change the course that your life will take.

The higher your compassion, love and tolerance, the higher will be your energetic field and the greater your powers. If you have great powers, you can get rid of the negative energetic fields of others through speech alone, just like Jesus did. He cured and purified people merely by saying a few words. If you possess higher powers, then through speech or just a single glance you can tap into those powers. For an ordinary person, however, their whole life is fixed and cannot be altered. You should be noble in character and have a pure heart and a moral nature. Follow the example of the heavenly principles[79] and through this conformity you can change the health prognosis of an inauspicious trigram or hexagram by changing your thoughts and in consequence your biological field and endocrine system. After such changes, how could a trigram or hexagram still yield the same result? When you possess high powers, you can resolve such karmic issues.

In the past, many teachers would use the so-called *sha* methods,[80] termination or killing methods, when an external energy had invaded the patient's body. But we should not employ them:

三界都親。

[Everything in] the three realms is kindred to us.[81]

We should only use three powers: those of love, compassion and forbearance. Everyone likes to go to temples, because only good things are spoken there and thus a positive atmosphere is created from that purity which can lead to a positive transformation of one's circumstances. Conversely, if someone is thinking negatively about something and you cast an inauspicious oracle on the matter, then you will just add further negative power and energy to the situation, and they will worry even more. You should always instil hope, even in a dire situation, to encourage a positive attitude and the strong motivation to overcome adversity, though without being misleading about the actual situation. The power of everyday words is not to be underestimated, to say nothing of chanting the scriptures and the special *gong*[82] of this, the so-called 'Following-the-Mouth Skill'.[83] When you possess such high skills, you say something and that makes it so. Thus, a bad oracle from the *Yi Jing* should be expressed to a person in a mitigated way, in combination with positivity, to avoid shattering them. Nevertheless, the urgency of changes to that person's lifestyle and the necessity of treatment should be relayed to them and not ignored. This ties in with the moral requirements of one who casts oracles. Without the positive powers of love, compassion and forbearance, how can you uplift someone? If you are selfish, how can you have such compassion and tolerance? These powers can manifest in one's speech even unintentionally in a moment that lacks awareness. When Tao Shifu[84] was studying in Shaanxi Province, in a temple called Louguan Tai,[85] there was a scripture master there – the priest in charge of the daily recitations of morning and evening scriptures[86] – and also another person who did odd jobs like cleaning and planting vegetables. He was not a Daoist renunciate. One morning after breakfast he talked about a bad dream he had had the previous night, which had left him feeling listless and fatigued. The scripture teacher joked that several ghosts had come to take him away. The helper fell to the ground in an instant and could not get up. Tao Shifu saw it all happen with her own eyes. Scripture reciters should not joke around, for the power of speech is inherent in their words.[87]

Regardless of your powers, whether they be those of speech or of accurate *Yi Jing* oracles and subsequent treatments, humility is paramount. Do not place yourself above anyone else or look condescendingly upon people. You must not think that because someone is on a different path to your own that their thoughts are on a lower level. Are they not also God's children? Each person has their own individual task and road to travel on. It may just be a matter of time for them before they walk the path. This world will never revolve around your wishes, blessings and prayers, however beautiful they may be. The greater your forbearance, the greater your love will be. Shakyamuni Buddha showed tolerance even to murderers.[88] Jesus forgave good people and sinners alike. Buddha had only eleven eminent disciples,[89] while Jesus had only twelve apostles, yet they were such great sages that they should have had the whole world as disciples.

If the deities, sages and spirits whom we pray to before our *Yi Jing* readings exist, then how are there still wars on this earth? There are demons in the Heavenly Kingdom[90] that come down from there to test us. In order to pass their tests, let go of your baggage, put it down. If you cannot put it down, then you will just have to grin and bear it. The demonic or negative energies exist at every level. Recently during the recitation of the morning scripture,[91] the spirit lamp[92] went out several times, while during the recitation of the evening scripture, the candle fell over twice. This gives you an idea of the presence and power of those energies. Take such negative energies[93] and turn them into positive ones. For if you just passively receive them, then they will become your own negative energies. To avoid this, cultivation is indispensable.

The Daoist sages and the masters of the *Yi Jing* in China were all produced by such a cultivation, and a process of refinement over time as they bear their yoke within society:

大浪淘沙。
Great waves wash out the sand.

To be a sage, you must grow up and mature in society.[94] If you feed steamed buns to a dog and it bites your hand, you cannot complain that this is not right, that you had good intentions. If you give somebody a knife and they say they will kill you unless you hand over your money, you cannot then cry and say that you had good intentions when you made the knife to be used for pre-paring feasts. This is called the 'Cultivation of the Dao' or the 'Cultivation of Refinement' within hardship, since no matter how pure-hearted you may be, you will not be exempt from challenges and injustices – these are all opportunities to improve your cultivation. Even though it is easy to live in a sheltered environment without challenges, like a five-star hotel, where you are given whatever you want, you will still have to pay a fee to dwell in this 'Heavenly Kingdom'. But my teachings of the *Yi Jing* are not for general sale, only with my permission can students attend courses with a tuition fee. If a certain troublesome student were to try to give me twenty-thousand Yuan,[95] I would not let that student stay at the temple any further since their thoughts and mine would no longer be aligned and at one, and so the connection between teacher and student would have to be severed. Once, due to their bad behaviour, I had to ask someone to leave after twenty days of tuition and I refunded the full amount that they had paid. That is why I look upon my students as a great family. One should never view any student as someone outside the family. Do you know how many times I have let students go in the past? Only rarely have I forsaken and lost students – it has happened no more than three or four times. However, in general terms, many prospective students are lost to teachers through being sent away like this. So do you understand the priceless value of being able to receive these teachings? There are approximately 6.8 million people living in Shiyan[96] and none of them will reprimand you.[97] If you are annoyed by someone who points out your faults like I do, then look for people like them, since none of them will tell you off when you are going astray. If someone reprimands and criticizes you, it means that they are close and related to you. Thus, in a family there is nothing that cannot be said. But in the city, people will just say 'very good' no matter what you do and will be very distant in their relations with you.

Change your thoughts! Take hold of your higher powers! This is what I require of you.

Q-A

In terms of karma, is it true that good things happen when you do good, and bad things happen when your deeds are bad?

You should just do what is good, because this is following the natural way and then you should not think about it afterwards at all. The bad things that you did in the past are like demons and when you do good deeds it is like slowly cleaning out those demons. They say that you need to perform three thousand good deeds in your lifetime.[98] Then you will have a foundation for cultivation. If you do virtuous things in order to be virtuous, this is not virtue.[99]

Does the casting of the oracle amalgamate different ideas into a general concept or are its workings unfathomable as a sacred mechanism?

I feel that my mind has gone blank, and I have lost all energy. Try not to use the method, but instead just approach your life with sincerity. With sincerity we can reach all the way to heaven. But you haven't attained that point yet. We can't reach the place of the sages who created these methods. But if you don't have sincerity, then you can use the *Yi Jing* method. Anybody can look at the *Yi Jing* text, though most people say that they don't understand it, that it doesn't make sense to them. Before you can have a really clear communication with the oracle deities, you need to have a method. If you don't have one, what you can do now is to be as sincere as you can or else use the *Yi Jing* method as well as you can. This is the best way to arrive at an accurate forecast.[100]

Does the Yi Jing operate at random or with a cohesive system of workings at its foundation?

The sentence I wrote on the board earlier – 'Quiet and unmoving, perceive [the *dao*] and succeed in communing with it' – represents the highest level of cultivation. This is because the hexagrams were created by higher beings whose knowledge came from a place of total connection between the above and below. What we are doing is like moving towards them from the bottom up, in the opposite direction. In this inverse way, we are going through these methods towards that higher place. So, when you cast an oracle, do you think that it is you who is casting the oracle?

Instead of the pebble?[101]

You do not need to state the obvious. So, when we were casting oracles before we had a teacher, we were using only our own agency, we were doing something ourselves. But now that I have opened the door for you and you belong to the lineage of teachers, they are all present when you cast a hexagram. They are all working in you. It is a little bit too soon to have told this to you,[102] but so as long as you have an honest and faithful heart, that's enough.

If, as a commoner, I cast hexagrams every day, does that bring bad karma to me?

We are all inside the great wheel of life and death. Everything is inside this book, the *Yi Jing*. What you use it for is a question of your inner moral qualities. High cultivators help others. If your cultivation is not high, then you cast oracles for your own self. Some people might ask, 'Can I rob a bank?'

Both the heavenly and earthly numbers[103] are calculable by adepts. Through the ten thousand ages, from ancient times until now, what has been hardest to fix are human thoughts; they go up to the heavens above and down into the earth below. The uprightness and rectitude of a noble person is required to turn bad things into good. If your thoughts are bad, then the good things in your life will also turn bad. If you cast hexagrams every day, that is not a problem. But really, one should only do so when inquiring about great matters. In the past, famous masters would in general cast hexagrams no more than once or twice a day and certainly not more than three times. When you are connected to heaven, you should certainly not use this for trivial things, for the spirits are always watching you. In Daoism it is said:

> 舉頭三尺有神明。
> Lift your head three *chi* and there will be
> spirit lights.[104]

CHAPTER TWO

易要求

YI JING REQUIREMENTS

THE *YI JING* requirements are comprised of rules and precepts. Everyone must know them. There is no alternative to this, which is why we use such methods to connect with the above, hoping to obtain clear information from it and notifications of auspiciousness or inauspiciousness, and success or failure. For any issue one should cast an oracle only once:

> 一事一斷。一事為主。
>
> A single casting with a single judgement becomes the main subject [of the oracle].

It is through being unobstructed in mind and through ceremonies that we obtain an accurate hexagram. One could draw parallels here with other ancient cultures such as the Mayans and many African cultures, which hold similar divinatory prayer ceremonies. Before any *Yi Jing* ritual that culminates in a hexagram can be held, there are nine requirements that should be met:

1. Sincerity or sincerity and faith 誠/誠信
2. Reverence 敬
3. Purification 潔
4. Solemnity 嚴
5. Stillness 靜
6. Incense 香
7. Prayers 禱
8. Shaking (of the hexagram) 搖
9. Gratitude 謝

1. One's sincerity must be vast and far-reaching. Without sincerity and faith, how might one connect with heaven?

2. Reverence means worship, or holding deities in the very highest esteem. If one is without reverence, there can be no connection with the higher realms.

3. Purification means that one must purify one's heart and one's body, and specifically one's mouth and hands, before each casting. Formerly in China, before dealing with great matters, for seven days in advance one would bathe and cleanse oneself as a means of self-transformation. To bathe and change into clean or even ritual clothing and to maintain a state of reverence for three days before an important undertaking was the minimum requirement back then. However, no one practises this today. Purification also includes the cleaning of one's altar

and the space where one practises *gong*. This is the purification of one's external environment. One also needs to purify oneself on the inside, such as the purification of one's mind. Ideally, during these three days at least, your thoughts and conduct must be pure in all affairs, whether major or minor. You must not think about anything bad or harmful, such as relationship issues or sexual matters, but must shut yourself off and remain alone. These principles of purification were also to be followed when casting oracles before major undertakings.[105]

In the great temple at Beijing, there is the Heavenly Altar[106] and the Earthly Altar.[107] The Heavenly Altar was built for heavenly sacrifices and the Earthly Altar for earthly sacrifices, offered in worship to the deities of heaven and the deities of earth respectively.

The Heavenly Altar[108] 天壇

To reach the heavens, sacrificial animals and precious objects like jade and silks were consumed by fire, while for the earth, red offerings were buried.[109] Such sacrifices to heaven and earth were performed for days before the official casting of hexagrams on issues of national importance. So now you can see how important such ceremonies are before casting an oracle.

4. Solemnity, strictness and sternness – this is not a game. You cannot say to yourself, 'I will dabble a little in the *Yi Jing*' and take it lightly. It is no joke. We must all want to perform the ceremonies and the casting of the oracle as well as possible each time we do so. Many of us often fail to comply with the procedure and the requirements, which produces a great deal of inconvenience and trouble for us.

5. Stillness – when approaching the altar, you must be still. Let us start by doing so now: note down a matter to inquire about from the *Yi Jing* and calm yourself for one minute. The goal is to commune with the above. In the past, the doctors of acupuncture and moxibustion would meditatively quieten their thoughts themselves before they inserted needles or applied moxibustion treatments.[110] This is what it means to comply with the rules. So focus your spirit and concentrate your mind, as though you were trying to catch hold of a snake or dragon. Give all your attention to this process, quieten your mind and body, and then synchronize your intent with your actions.

6. The offering of incense – nowadays, you can also practise *Yi Jing* divination without incense. In the past, however, this was a must. But it may be inconvenient in some circumstances.[111] This would not be a problem, as this is a flexible rule:

心通法自通。

When the heart-mind communicates, the laws
communicate by themselves.

When one's mind is free and unobstructed, it can be flexible.
But if one does make an offering of incense, this should be
either one or three incense sticks – no one offers two. This
order for placing three incense sticks is as follows (if only
one stick is used, then step two and three can obviously be
omitted): firstly, the three incense sticks are held in one's
right hand. The first incense stick is held between the middle
finger and thumb and placed in the incense bowl; the second
stick is placed by positioning the first incense stick within the
hole formed by the ring finger and thumb holding the second,
which places the second stick on the right; the third stick is
placed on the other side by holding it between the index finger
and thumb. The incense sticks should be placed one *cun* or a
thumb's width apart. All of the incense sticks should be per-
fectly straight, vertical and level with each other.[112] This is to
be followed every time there is an offering of incense. It is an
essential part of the sincerity, reverence, solemnity and communion required. Then, having lit the incense, one prays.

7. Prayers. What form should one's prayers take? How should
    one pray? There are special incantations for this very purpose:

弟子〇〇〇今天為了【... 事情】虔誠叩請

伏羲神農文王周公孔聖乾坎艮震巽離坤兌八卦
大神占卦童子翻卦郎君為弟子一八八六十四
卦方法下賜。一卦以示 吉凶禍福。弟
子〇〇〇虔誠叩拜起卦。

*Dìzi 000 jīntiān wèile [... shìqíng] qiánchéng kòuqǐng fúxī
shénnóng wénwáng zhōugōng kǒngshèng qián kan gěn zhèn
xùn lí kūn duì bāguà dàshén zhānguà tóngzǐ fānguà láng
jūn wèi dìzǐ yī bābā liùshísì guà fāngfǎ xiàsì. Yīguà yǐshì
jíxiōng huòfú. Dìzǐ 000 qiánchéng kòubài qǐguà.*

Today this disciple [insert your name],[113] for [the sake
of this oracle], piously and sincerely prostrate themselves and begs Fu Xi, the Divine Farmer, King Wen,
the Duke of Zhou, the Sage Kong, the great spirits
of the eight trigrams, *qian, kan, gen, zhen, xun, li,
kun,* and *dui,* the Hexagram-Casting Infant and the
Hexagram-Everting Husband to confer down to the
disciple the formula by one of the eight-eight, sixty-
four, hexagrams. One such hexagram will allow to
demonstrate auspiciousness or inauspiciousness,
fortune or misfortune.

This disciple [insert your name] piously and sincerely
prostrates themselves and casts the hexagram.[114]

At the place where you insert your name, this should be your name in Chinese. Shiqing [... 事情] denotes the matter that you are inquiring about, which can take many forms. It might be about travel, building a house, seeking a boyfriend or girlfriend, employment prospects, and many other issues. The Hexagram-Casting Infant and the Hexagram-Everting Husband are the spiritual helpers of the casting, the so-called Casting-Hexagrams-Spirits. The phrase *wei dizi yi baba liushisi gua fangfa xiasi* 為弟子一八八六十四卦方法下賜[115] refers to those spirits above who give a hexagram to the human person below. *Yigua yishi jixiong huofu* means 'give me a sign as to whether this matter will be met with success or failure'. In other words, 'Tell me if this matter is auspicious or inauspicious'. After you have said this, you can cast your hexagram. Then you pray, and you should maintain this reverential attitude towards the deities for the rest of your lifetime.

There is also an incantatory text for when you are learning how to perform the casting method. Then you should recite the following sentence:

弟子在學習起卦諸神退位。
Dìzǐ zài xuéxí qǐ guà zhū shén tuìwèi.
This disciple is learning to cast hexagrams.
May all spirits step aside from their posts.

Or:

弟子實習諸神退位。
Dìzǐ shíxí zhū shén tuìwèi.
This disciple is putting [the method of casting] into practice. May all spirits step aside from their posts.

Or:

弟子練習諸神退位。

Dìzǐ liànxí zhū shén tuìwèi.

This disciple is performing [the exercise of casting].
May all spirits step aside from their posts.

Alternatively, before the casting you can recite the following
invocation:

眼觀青天，奉請師傅在身邊。弟子〇〇〇虔誠焚
香，叩請乾坎艮震巽離坤兌八卦大神，叩請伏
羲神農文王周公孔聖歷代先師卦師、占卦童子、
翻卦郎君，叩請弟子本尊上界上師恩師度師，
弟子〇〇〇有請敬畏〇〇〇，叩請祖師一八純卦
【八八六十四卦】，下賜一卦，一事吉凶禍福。

*Yǎn guān qīngtiān, fèng qǐng shīfù zài shēnbiān, dìzǐ XXX
qiánchéng fénxiāng, kòuqǐng qián kǎn gèn zhèn xùn lí
kūn duì bāguà dàshén, kòu qǐng fúxī shénnóng wénwáng
zhōugōng kǒng shèng lìdài xiānshī guà shī, zhāngguà tóngzǐ,
fān guà láng jūn, kòu qǐng dìzǐ běnzūn shàngjiè shàngshī
ēnshī dùshī, dìzǐ momomo yǒu qǐng jìngwèi XXX, kòu qǐng
zǔshī yībā chúnguà [bābāliùshísì guà], xiàcì yí guà, yí shì
jíxiōng huòfú.*

Observing the clear sky, with respect I beseech the
masters to be by my side. The disciple [insert your name],
piously and sincerely burns incense, prostrates
themselves and beseeches the great spirits of the eight
trigrams: qian, kan, gen, zhen, xun, li, kun, dui.

[This disciple] prostrates themselves and beseeches
Fu Xi, the Divine Farmer, King Wen, the Duke of
Zhou, Sage Kong [Zi], the past masters and divination
masters of previous generations, the Hexagram-
Divining Infants[116] and the Hexagram-Everting
Gentlemen. [This disciple] prostrates themselves and
beseeches the Original Honoured One of this disciple,[117]
the High Masters from the High Realms, the Graceful
Masters and the Masters of Deliverance. This disciple
[insert your name], beseeches [the masters] with
reverence for [the sake of the subject matter[118] of this
oracle], prostrates themselves and beseeches the
ancestral masters that one of the eight pure trigrams
[/one of the eight [times] eight, sixty-four hexagrams][119]
be conferred down [to them],[120] the one trigram[121]
[/hexagram][122] through which [the disciple] will be able
to [divine] the matter [about which he is inquiring],
whether it will be auspicious or inauspicious,
[and whether it will bring] fortune or misfortune.

8. Shake the hexagram.[123] After that, the practical aspect of the
oracle has been completed.

9. Express gratitude:

弟子 〇〇〇 虔誠叩謝再拜。
Dìzǐ XXX qiánchéng kòuxiè zàibài.
This disciple [insert your name] piously and
sincerely prostrates themselves to express gratitude
in full obeisance.

This is the process by which one says 'Thank You' to the higher realms. Alternatively, you can say:

弟子 OOO 虔誠叩拜。

Dìzǐ XXX qiánchéng kòubài.

This disciple [insert your name] piously and sincerely prostrates themselves.

Or:

弟子 OOO 虔誠再拜。

Dìzǐ XXX qiánchéng zàibài.

This disciple [insert your name] piously and sincerely prostrates themselves again.

This is an expression of piety and respect. If you do not have an altar, then simply face north. But the table on which you perform the casting must be clean. You must place the things[124] you will use on the table with great care.

CHAPTER THREE

LEGENDS AND STORIES

BY LI SHIFU

GOATS IN THE ATTIC[125]

A LESSON CAN BE learned from events that once took place in Huanjiapo, a village which lies at the very bottom of White Horse Mountain, downhill from the electricity line from Zhuangjiapo. One household owned almost thirty goats and one day they were unable to find them. They searched everywhere. Eventually they discovered the goats beyond the south gate on White Horse Mountain – but only twenty-four goats remained, so they had lost four goats, the equivalent of a whole year's income. They looked for the remaining four goats for a long time without success. Subsequently, they asked me to cast a *Yi Jing* oracle to help them find the goats. I cast the li trigram and it seemed that they would run into someone wearing red clothes in a southerly direction, where the goats would be recovered upstairs above a building.[126] But how could the goats be upstairs in an attic?

I instructed them: 'Look tomorrow in this southern direction and you will encounter a middle-aged woman in red clothes who is working.' The next morning, between *chen* and *si* time,[127] the villagers went out to search. They went over the mountain and bumped into a woman, who was working on the ground. 'Have you seen our goats? We're from White Horse Mountain.' The woman replied that around a week to ten days earlier, four large goats had come over the mountain. Some people had pulled them away. All of the villagers were her neighbours, so she knew the house that had taken the goats. 'Go over there and ask that family. They have your goats.' When they approached the house and inquired about the goats, one of the family members said: 'I killed them, because I didn't have the means to herd them for a long time. After killing them, I hung them from the roof of the house.' So, they had finally tracked down their goats. 'You killed our goats!', they cried, and an argument ensued. 'We need compensation!', they demanded. The man replied: 'I herded and fed them for days on end and still you want money from me?' 'You killed our goats, so you must compensate us.' The culprit asked: 'Who told you where to find your goats?' They answered: 'A Daoist who lives on top of the mountain.' So in the end I got caught up in their dispute.

This was the first of three conflicts that were caused by divinations.[128] As with this example, arguments especially arise from oracles involving a search for lost items. So later on, although many people would seek me out to cast an oracle for them, I would say to them: 'I do not know the art of divination.' They would then implore of me: 'I haven't been able to find something for a long time, please can you calculate an oracle just a little bit?' But when you are very clear in your divination, it leads to arguments. So you have to say: 'It might be in this direction, or it might be in that one.' You have to calculate poorly so they cannot locate it. If you cast badly, people will stop seeking you out.

THE SOLITARY NEIGHBOUR

Immortal Paradise Rock at the north side of Heavenly Horse Peak

THE SECOND STORY involves a house at the back of the mountain. When you stand on the large Immortal Paradise[129] Rock by the Jade Temple, you can see that house. The man who lives there had lost an item of clothing and came to ask me to cast a divination in order to retrieve it. The oracle revealed that the thing in question had been taken by his neighbour, an old man who had given it to his daughter. I did not remember that this man lived at the back of the mountain. In the vicinity of the man's house there was only one other household, situated in front of it to the northwest, and inhabited by a man and his daughter. I had never visited this area, since there were only two homes there. If the man had

had two neighbours, then I would not have known who stole the item. But since there was only one other house there, the culprit was clear. The man confronted his neighbour, crying out: 'You stole it!' 'No, I didn't!' the neighbour replied. Then they came up the mountain together to see me, since it was I, Daoist Li of the Five Immortals Temple, who had made the claim. I was still in a good position to refute any accusations of personal involvement, since I had a record of the cast showing that it was the oracle, not me, that had made the prediction.

'You called me a thief!', the man reproached me. So I retorted: 'When did I say those words? My prediction was as follows: "A man has lost some clothing; the *qian* trigram with a third changing line was cast. An old man took it and gave it to his daughter." This prediction caused me a tremendous amount of aggravation, since the man had blamed his neighbour directly as a consequence of it. But I told them that I had never mentioned any names. However, I had known that it was the old man, because there was just one girl living in his home and they were a poor family. 'I didn't say that he stole it', I insisted. But they continued to argue and dispute in the main temple. It was a terrible headache. 'You stole it!' 'No, I didn't!' Eventually, they left. Less than half a year later the person who had lost the item came back and said that he had found it, and that it was his neighbour who had stolen it for his daughter. My castings have created several disputes like this. With lost items, if you name the thief, it leads to quarrels and conflicts. Stolen property is a matter for the law – we do not have the authority to act in this way.

The Family Feud

THE PEOPLE IN this story are still around here. One is outside right now, he's the big man who sells incense in the front of the temple. At one time he had lost his cow and could not find it. The man and his wife searched for a long time in vain. In the countryside a cow amounts to half of a family's property and income. They could not find it anywhere. So they approached me to help them. I had an oracle cast and obtained the *qian* trigram, which revealed that the cow could be found in the north-west. Furthermore, it was by the water and had been taken by someone close and related to them, who was now looking after it. This person was a man who fed it grass, was between fifty and sixty years old, and was very thin. While the husband was still pondering the oracle and had not yet begun to search again, two people came looking for cows to buy. A few days before the cow went missing, a butcher had come to a relative of the man, called Da Pingzi, also looking to buy cows. Therefore, the man and his wife strongly suspected the relative of selling their cow.[130] His home was the highest house in Zhangjiapo below Taishan Temple, the temple mid-way up the mountain, though he has since moved. The farmer and his wife confronted the man: 'Did you steal our cow?' 'No, I didn't', he replied. 'When do you think I might have stolen your cow? Who said so?' 'Elder Li[131] from the Five Immortals Temple said it.'

So they all came up to the temple together. Fortunately, I still had the paper on which the oracle had been written. 'What has this to do with me?' I asked them. 'I never mentioned anyone's name. I have shown you what I wrote. Did I ever say you stole the cow? Go and look for it.' I showed them the trigram and pinned it on the wall. 'You still need to look for it in the north-west', I said to them. They had been arguing about the matter for two whole hours at the temple, but at these words they stopped. Where did the cow go? It had run off around the mountain, next to the water. And this turned out to be precisely correct. On the path to the Yellow Dragon Village, someone had found the cow and handed it over to the police. They tried to find the owner but did not succeed. As they could not have it tied up in the police station, they gave it to someone to look after and feed it, who lived next to the river. This happened to be the second cousin of the cow's owner, a skinny man who was more than fifty years old. In the end the owner led it back from the police but was told to give his cousin some compensation for the care it had received. Although the farmer gave me some cigarettes for my help,[132] he argued with his cousin over the compensation money.

Therefore, you should not cast for lost property! It will lead to arguments and strife. You might get someone imprisoned and then the family members will give you trouble for incarcerating that person. My oracles have led to three such disputes in the past, so I no longer cast them. An arrogant and conceited attitude – 'My oracles are so accurate!' – will create selfishness and a desire for wealth and fame. Instead, we should move towards the light and show compassion and forbearance. We should be good to others and of help to society, bringing people together rather than creating division between them. We should not act only for ourselves. Our moral behaviour dictates how we should use the Yi Jing:

君子得之固窮，小人得之輕命。

Noble people obtain [knowledge of the *dao*],
whereas low people learn [about the *dao*], they only
take lightly their life-destiny.[133]

A good person applies their wisdom in order to assist people, to
express their love and tolerance. A lowly person does things only
for personal gain and is very selfish. If you learn the *Yi Jing*, you
should ask how this might benefit others? You can accumulate
wealth on a material level without any elevation of your spiritual
nature. This will affect you in a very negative way and you will lose
more and more of your compassion. Eventually, everything you
do will be for selfish purposes alone.

IMMINENT DEATH

A N ORACLE WAS once cast for a man which prophesied that he would die within two hours at the bottom of a mountain. But since he was far away from the nearest mountain, so he puzzled over the meaning of this divination. It would have taken him a whole day to get to the bottom of a mountain, or at least seven or eight hours by car. However, less than two hours later he was crushed by a roof that caved in. This part of the roof is called a 'mountain roof'.[134] When interpreting an oracle, a word like 'mountain' does not have to be a physical feature like the Himalayas or White Horse Mountain. It can also refer to its resonances in language – for example, there is a city in America called 'Bygone Gold Mountain'.[135] So be careful not to dismiss an oracle that you receive.

METAL ABOVE – WOOD BELOW

THIS STORY CONCERNS a master of divination who lived in the Tang Dynasty and used the Apricot Blossom Method.[136] One night, his neighbour knocked on his door. Why was he knocking so late, the master and his wife wondered. It was between six and seven o'clock in the evening.[137] The man quickly threw an oracle to find out why his neighbour was calling on him at such an hour. The oracle said he had come to borrow something that was 'Metal above, wood below'.[138] The husband said that this must stand for a knife or an axe, while his wife suggested that it might also represent a hoe.[139] The celestial time[140] was around dinner; it was certainly not time for work. Then, they opened the door and their neighbour explained that he needed an axe to chop some firewood to cook his dinner.[141]

This story is about the principle of time and, in particular, the needs of a specific time. At noon people are usually eating, while at night people are sleeping – this refers to times when the vast majority of people are doing the same thing. However, there might be someone who guards the land and fields at night while most are sleeping. Or some people might be fasting at a time when most are eating. How can one take such exceptions into account when interpreting an oracle? This is what is meant by the principle of the celestial time and the natural order of heaven. If I am living in the Himalayas, then how could I die by the sea? How could my pet drown in the ocean? Although these oracles may seem puzzling in their immediate context, they will make sense when the celestial time is fulfilled. People plant vegetables in the spring and in the summer work in the fields, so why would someone be out in the snow cutting wood?[142] To act according to customs and social convention during the seasons and days is called the 'principle of heaven and earth' or the 'human principle'. Therefore, oracles should be based on such customs, habits and common sense in their predictions, rather than the oddities of people going against such principles.[143]

THE BATTLE OF THE RED CLIFF[144]

Romance of the Three Kingdoms[145]

ZHUGE LIANG[146] WAS ordered to make one hundred thousand arrows in three days. Since it was impossible to perform such a feat, he cast an oracle which revealed that a great mist would arise. There was a great deal at stake since he had been told that if he did not succeed, he would be killed. So he had to borrow the arrows from his enemy. He placed straw figures on boats as he approached the enemy's camp by water and created a loud clamour as a ruse so the enemy would think it was a large fleet in attack. Since the enemy could not see anything due to the thick mist obscuring their view, they shot salves of arrows aimlessly in front of them, piercing what were only straw men, and thus the arrows fell into Zhuge Liang's hands without any loss of life. [147]

VIOLATING THE HEAVENLY LAW[148]

The Dragon King Wrecking Yuan Shoucheng's Shop[149]

THERE IS A very famous story in *The Journey to the West* about Yuan Shoucheng, the uncle of Founding Ancestor Yuan Tiangang,[150] who designed the grave for Empress Wu Zetian in Shaanxi, which has not yet been opened up by archaeologists.[151] He was very accurate in his casting of oracles. Each day on the street he would cast three times only – once for each meal. That was enough for him. He could forecast when and how much it would rain. The rain would start and stop as if he had conjured it himself. It so happened that an old fisherman had become unable to catch any fish. So he asked the diviner: 'Where should I fish?' Through his divinatory skill, Yuan Shoucheng was able to tell him the most auspicious location for fishing. Thus, the fisherman was able to find a great many fish there and caught a large number of them every day which made him very happy. He gave the diviner one carp each day to express his gratitude. This continued day after day and after a while he thought to himself, 'I have only one net.' So he made ten more nets. Desire had taken hold of him and he scooped up a lot of fish. But the Dragon King[152] was not happy about this: 'Every day he is taking the lives of my kinsfolk[153] by throwing his nets in our home.' The fisherman was looking for trouble by killing so many fish.[154] Thus, the Dragon King, a water spirit, transformed himself into a human being in order to obtain a divination from Yuan Shoucheng. He said to him: 'I have come today to ask when it is going to rain, and how much it will rain and for how long?' In exchange for some money, Yuan Shoucheng performed the divination. 'It will rain tomorrow and for two hours. The rain will fall from 11am to 1pm, and there will be thunder at 12.20pm.'

In fact, the water spirit, the Dragon King, was in charge of the water and rain, and he could command how much it would rain. So he knew what to do in order to stop all the life in the water from being killed. As the administrator of rain, he was aware of when it was going to rain and in what quantity. However, the one who was truly in charge of the heavenly *qi*[155] at the very top of the hierarchy was the Great Jade Emperor,[156] who handed down his mandate to the Dragon King. Nevertheless, the Dragon King ordered that it should rain later than Yuan Shouheng had predicted,[157] and though he had divined that there would be enough rain to fill half a cup, the quantity was altered to be much less. Instead of finishing at 1pm as predicted, the rain actually stopped half an hour earlier.

The Dragon King stormed back to Yuan Shoucheng and fiercely complained: 'Your casting was wrong! Give me my money back!' And he smashed up his stall in anger. Then Yuan Shoucheng cast an oracle to discover the real identity of this person.[158] He saw that it was the Dragon King. Then he said cooly to him: 'This spells trouble for you, we have fought here, but it is you who will receive the punishment from heaven. You disobeyed the orders of the Jade Emperor, who will have your head cut off.' And this is what happened in the end.[159]

LIVE TO BE A HUNDRED!

A NINETY-NINE-YEAR-OLD LADY WHO lived at the back of White Horse Mountain was given an oracle by the man who comes to our temple during Daoist festivals with a little trigram stand.

Daoist Diviner during the Festival of the Birthday of the Five Immortals

He cast a *Yi Jing* oracle for her which predicted that she would have only three more months to live. The old lady's second daughter was very filial and devoted to her mother and wanted to expand her life to more than a hundred years of age. So she repeated the casting with other diviners and they all yielded the same result: her mother had three months left to live. Thus, she came here to Five Immortals Temple to try to avert the prediction.[160] Her mother lived on for five months, rather than three, and I told her jokingly to go back and break the fortune-teller's trigram table. This is actually a true story.[161] Therefore, some things cannot be forecast. Never say that a prediction is fixed and for certain or you might end up getting in trouble.

ENDNOTES

[1] Photo credit: Christina Chandler.

[2] Some sources believe there to be three versions of the *Yi Jing*: The *Lianshan* 連山, literally 'Connecting Mountains', of the Xia Dynasty, the *Guicang* 歸藏, literally 'Return to the Storehouse', of the Shang Dynasty, and the *Yi [Jing] of the Zhou [Dynasty]* (*Zhouyi* 周易). While the last is fully preserved, the first is only preserved in fragments (see Edward Shaughnessy, *Unearthing the Changes: Recently Discovered Manuscripts of the Yi Jing (I Ching) and Related Texts*) and the second is completely lost. Other scholars argue that there is only one true Yi Jing, the *Yi [Jing] of the Zhou [Dynasty]*, and consider the other two be distinct and separate divination systems, only related to the Yi through sharing the principles of the hexagram. The translators have adopted the former stance and all mention of the Yi Jing is to be equated with the *Yi [Jing] of the Zhou [Dynasty]*.

[3] Zhuangzi was a pivotal figure in Classical Daoism who lived in the late 4th century BCE. The text bearing his name is a compilation of writings ascribed to him.

[4] In Chinese, 四書 [*sishu*], which include *The Analects [of Confucius]* (*Lunyu* 論語), *The Great Learning* (*Daxue* 大學), *The Doctrine of the Mean* (*Zhongyong* 中庸) and the *Mengzi* (孟子).

[5] In Chinese, 五經 [*wujing*], which are the *Yi Jing* 易經, *The Esteemed Documents* (*Shangshu* 尚書), also known as *The Book of Documents* (*Shujing* 書經), *The Book of Poems* (*Shijing* 詩經), *The Record of Rites* (*Liji* 禮記) and *The Spring and Autumn [Annals]* (*Chunqiu* 春秋).

[6] The binary principle of the *Yi Jing* is reliant on yin lines, which are broken, and yang lines, which are solid. By combining these two into the stacking up of six lines, sixty four hexagrams can be created. Interestingly it is also known that Gottfried Wilhelm Leibniz (1646–1716), the famous German mathematician, philosopher, religious thinker and inventor of the binary code in 1679, had access to the Yi Jing. On the one hand, it is widely believed that through his correspondence with Father Joachim Bouvet (1650–1730), a Jesuit in China, Leibniz was exposed to the work of Shao Yong (1011–1070), who had re-arranged the 64 hexagrams into what is called 'Fu Xi's Sixty-Four Hexagrams Sequence'(*fuxi liushisigua*

cixu 伏羲六十四卦次序), and that therefore this led to the creation of the binary system. See also https://www.biroco.com/yijing/fuxis-creen.htm for the entire sequence and https://www.biroco.com/yijing/sequence.htm for an animated illustration of how the hexagrams transform. Up until this point the hexagrams were said to be arranged in the King Wen Wang sequence, which has been frequently criticized by scholars past and present for being random and arbitrary (a third arrangement was devised by Jing Fang (77–37 BCE), which is crucial for the Six Lines Method of this book). See also József Drasny, 'The Regular Grouping of the Hexagrams before the Yi jing - The King Wen Groups', and Gabrielle Felley, 'Yintelligence: The Mapping of the Pre-Heaven or FuXi Hexagrams to the Post-Heaven or King Wen Hexagrams'. On the other hand, attention has also been drawn to a letter fromLeibniz to Bouvet in 1703, i.e. after his invention of the binary code, in which he writes of the *Yi Jing*:

> … it is a very surprising thing that it perfectly matches my new manner of arithmetic and that I should have written you about my arithmetic at just the appropriate time, that is, just when you were applying yourself to the decipherment of these lines.

See also Alan Berkowitz and Daniel Cook, 'Letter J: 18 May 1703; Leibniz to Bouvet', Frank Swetz, 'Leibniz, the Yijing, and the Religious Conversion of the Chinese', James Ryan, 'Leibniz' Binary System and Shao Yong's "Yijing"', Karl Flieder, 'The Yijing – The Philosophical Foundation of the Binary System?' and Jerry Lodder, 'Binary Arithmetic: From Leibniz to von Neumann'.

[7] The character 易 [*yi*] 'change' combines 'sun' 日 [*ri*] above with 'do not' or 'nothing' 勿 [*wu*], while the latter is commonly interpreted as representing the moon. Thus, the alternation and fluctuations of the sun and moon symbolize cosmological changes. In dualistic Chinese philosophy the upper component would be considered representative of the *yang* principle while the lower component signifies the *yin* principle. *The Explanations of Scripts and Explications of Characters* (*Shuowen Jiezi* 說文解字) provides an alternative interpretation of this character:

> 易 :蜥易，蝘蜓，守宮也。象形。《祕書》說 :日月為易，象陰陽也。

> *Yi* means 'changeable lizard', 'predator of cicadas', and 'palace guardian' [i.e. the three different Chinese names for a gecko – it is called "palace guardian" in the western regions, 'changeable lizard' when it is found in grassland, and 'predator of cicadas'

when on a wall]. It is a pictograph. *The Secret Book* says: 'The sun and the moon [combine together] to become *Yi*, as an image of *yin* and *yang*.'

[8] This sentence points to the orbiting of the planets; just as the sun and moon rise and set in the firmament within one day and night, so all sentient beings undergo a process from birth to death.

[9] See endnote 6. In *The Mandate of Heaven: Hidden History in the I Ching*, chapter 2, 'The Title of the Oracle', Steven Marshall dedicates an entire chapter to the provenance of the character for 'Changes'. Most insightfully, he reveals that it was linked to sacrifices to the sun, and thus possibly depicts the sun peeking out from behind a cloud with three rays of light piercing through it. It can, therefore, be speculated that the character itself was part of a ritual to invoke good weather and clear the sky for the sun to emerge once more.

[10] Qin Shihuang 秦始皇 (259–210 BCE), was the founder of the Qin dynasty and the first emperor of a unified China.

[11] The Yellow River Map (*hetu* 河圖) and the River Luo Scroll (*luoshu* 洛書) are first mentioned in the *The Esteemed Documents* (*Shangshu* 尚書), from around the time of the Shang and Zhou dynasties, in the chapter 'Testimonial Charge' (*guming* 顧命). There is some ambiguity as to whether today's map and scroll, which can be traced back to the Song Dynasty, are the same as those described below in the *Yi [Jing] of the Zhou [Dynasty]* (*Zhouyi* 周易):

河出圖，洛出書，聖人則之。易有四象，所以示也。繫辭焉，所以告也。定之以吉凶，所以斷也。

The map came out of the Yellow River and the scroll came out of the Luo River, and the sages imitated them.

Through the four images [i.e. real images 實象, metaphorical images 假象, conceptual images 義象, and applicable images 用象], the *Yi [Jing]* is able to instruct us regarding [their sagacious principles]. Through the 'Appended Sayings', it informs us on each [of the four images]. Thus, to determine whether something is auspicious or inauspicious, it is [the *Yi Jing*] that [enables one to] make a judgment.

The four images are fundamentally a categorization of the 'Commentary on the Image' allegedly written by Confucius. Whereas 'real images' [*zhenxiang* 實象] refers to hexagram images that correspond to natural phenomena, 'metaphorical (or false) images' [*jiaxiang* 假象] refers to abstract hexagram images with no corresponding natural phenomena;

'conceptual images' [*yixiang* 義象] refers to the concepts and ideas that each hexagram image represents, while 'applicable image' [*yongxiang* 用象] refers to how one applies such concepts. Furthermore, it has been argued that the Yellow River Map was a kind of jade stone, which had a texture that was interpreted to represent the eight trigrams. See also Sun Yanzhe, 'The Interpretation of Hetu and Luoshu'.

[12] Li Shifu implies that such a fiery animal might have been a flying saucer misidentified by ancient human beings who were unable to recognize such a futuristic machine.

[13] According to a legendary tale from the Han Dynasty, a dragon horse, a dragon's head with a horse's body, emerged from the He river bearing the circular numerical marks from which Fu Xi deduced the eight trigrams in their pre-heaven sequence. Of the exact procedure nothing has been recorded, not even in the classics, though the He River Map is mentioned in *The Analects [of Confucius]*. However, what is in use nowadays can only reliably be traced back to the Song Dynasty.

[14] In essence some *Yi Jing* methods such as the Six Lines Method and the Plum Blossom Art rely on the calendrical system of China, which is comprised of the Ten Heavenly Stems and the Twelve Earthly Branches in a sexagesimal cycle.

[15] This refers to each stem and branch as well as each trigram being assigned a specific number.

[16] In Chinese, 陰符經 [*yinfu jing*].

[17] In Chinese, 六爻 [*liuyao*], which is the method laid out in this book.

The Six Lines Method dispenses with any line or hexagram text and thus does not rely on the *Yi Jing* text (or a translation of it). In order to be able to employ such a method, the six lines need to be mapped with the five phases and the six relatives, and also compared with the phases of the particular earthly branch of the day and month at the time of casting. Furthermore, there are other five phases-related interactions of the lines of the original hexagram with the lines of the transformed hexagram, which comes into being from a numerically calculated moving line, i.e. a yin line changes into a yang line and vice versa. For example, supporting or controlling, as well as the use of the seven animal spirits or beasts, which have certain meanings associated with them in terms of auspiciousness and inauspiciousness as well as causes of disease, all of which enable a finer accuracy in one's reading. The style taught in this book also does not rely on the throwing of yarrow stalks or tossing of coins to build a hexagram, but hinges purely on the calendrical eight characters at the moment of casting one's hexagram.

[18] This is a Chinese currency, 1/100th of one Yuan.

[19] Li Shifu hints here at all his worldly commitments as abbot of a temple and member of the local and district Daoist associations. Daoism in general advocates that one be secluded and removed from the bustle of society to pursue one's higher cultivation after a phase within society, preferably in a cave in the deep forest on a remote mountain.

[20] In order to obtain a hexagram, one must add the pertaining numbers of the eight characters at the time of casting. This is an important point of difference from the coin toss or the yarrow stalk method, which is also sometimes called the milfoil stalk method. The Six Lines Method therefore is also classified as a numerological method.

[21] Li Shifu stresses here that the high sages do not need to resort to coin tossing or time-based calculations as they have access to the *Yi Jing*'s answers regardless. It is also said that high sages should not seek to avoid difficult circumstances through divining, but should instead seek the *dao* within 'bitterness' or austerity, which then transforms it into something else. Li Shifu himself does not use the *Yi Jing* anymore as far as I could witness in my years of living at the temple, and he fends off guests and friends who seek *Yi Jing* readings by feigning not to know enough about the subject or having forgotten how to use it. Only after repeated prodding by his senior students did he agree to teach it and commented that he could then delete it from his memory to create more space on his brain's 'hard drive'. There was only one occasion on which he asked me to do a reading for a visitor with a serious liver disease, in order to make a prognosis. After I had calculated the hexagram and proposed that the chances of a complete recovery were almost nil, he checked the correctness of my reading and nodded, thus silently confirming the grim outlook.

[22] Literally, 'flower bean'.

[23] At this point Li Shifu went on briefly to discuss the story 'Metal Above – Wood Below' which appears in 'Legends and Stories'; for these comments, see endnote 139.

[24] The more unobstructed one's connection is to the higher realms and the deities in charge of *Yi Jing* divination, as invoked by the incantations listed in a later chapter, the more accurate one's divination will be, even if one has calculated wrongly.

[25] Cheng Tong, one of Li Shifu's senior Western students, can attest to this. Once he examined a hexagram from a previous divination by Li Shifu that had turned out to be very accurate and noticed a mistake had been made in the mathematical calculations that formed it.

[26] Li Shifu at this point went into a brief excursus on the importance of having a physical body in the third dimension:

Without a physical body, on what boat could you travel across to the other shore? Without a body, what ladder would you have to ascend to heaven? For one month I chanted the Daoist scriptures for one of my students from Mount Wuduo 五朵山 in Nanyang, who had jumped off a cliff [i.e. who had thus lost his body or boat]. I do not know who my student's other teachers were.

[27] Li Shifu here warns against the temptation to charge exorbitant sumsof money for *Yi Jing* readings, which will lead to a loss of one'sorientation in line with the *dao*, which should be directed towards reducing suffering and disease.

[28] The four pillars (*sizhu* 四柱) and eight characters (*bazi* 八字) form a system that is frequently applied in *fengshui* and astrological prognostications such as birth charts. The name stems from the four pairs, each pair consisting of one heavenly stem and one earthly branch, one pair each for the year, the month, the day and the hour, which means that stems and branches can be repeated and not all stems and branches can appear. It is also crucial for any *Yi Jing* method that is based on numerology.

[29] The ten heavenly stems and the twelve earthly branches are part of the Chinese calendrical system; each day is allocated a stem and a branch in this sexagesimal cycle. 'Mutual unification' refers to the generating cycle (*xiangsheng* 相生) of the five phases.

[30] The eight trigrams have allocated or assigned numbers in both their pre-heaven and post-heaven arrangements.

[31] The pre-heaven and post-heaven arrangements refer to the eight trigrams and their respective positions in the eight directions. The supporting and controlling cycles depict the relationship of the five phases based on observations of nature, e.g. earth controls water just like a dam hems in a river. The transforming and unification cycles are more elaborate concepts regarding the interaction between phases. The insulting cycle is the reverse of the controlling cycle wherein the supposedly controlled phase turns against the controlling phase as it possesses a relative excess of strength.

[32] A trigram consists of three lines, which can be either *yin* or *yang*, thereby creating eight different trigrams, *qian, zhen, kan, gen, kun, xun, li*, and *dui*.

[33] The Gregorian calendar is calculated by the movement of the sun and thus is also called the solar calendar, with a month being either 30 or 31 days, while the lunar calendar, as the name suggests, is based on the lunar cycle, with the first day of each month representing the new moon and the 15th day the full moon, with each month being either 29 or 30 days long. While the Gregorian calendar employs a leap year, the lunar or farmers' calendar uses an intercalary month roughly every three years, which means that there are thirteen lunar months in that given year by repeating one month in its numbering.

[34] The twenty-eight constellations [*ershiba xiu* 二十八宿] are constellations of the Chinese astrological system that derive from the moon cycles and divide the sky into four quadrants of seven constellations each. The yellow path [*huangdao* 黃道] and the black path [*heidao* 黑道] are folkloric terms for auspicious and inauspicious dates respectively. The former borrows its name from the earth's orbit around the sun (yellow) while the latter is considered retrograde.

[35] This conversion involves the transfer of a western date into the eastern date of the four pillars and eight characters. This is commonly done by consulting a 10,000 year calendar, yet there are mathematical equations that enable one to do this through mental calculations alone. While this book will provide the memory method for the sake of completeness, it is by no means deemed a requirement by Li Shifu.

[36] In Chinese 梅花易數 [*meihua yishu*], which is comprised of two methods. The first is a combination of the date and a random event observed by the casting diviner, and the second method is to intuit two objects during the divination and then to interpret the first of these as the upper trigram and the second as the lower trigram. It is said to have been invented by Shao Yong 邵雍 (1011–1077) in the Song Dynasty.

[37] In Chinese, 鐵板神書 [*tieban shenshu*]. It consists of 12,000 lines of text and is ascribed to Shao Yong 邵雍 (1011–1077), a Song Dynasty cosmologist and philosopher who was crucial in the development of the Neo-Confucian school.

[38] I.e. the current president of the People's Republic of China.

[39] This is better known as Kung Fu.

⁴⁰ *Gongfu* compassion ties in with martial virtue [*wude* 武德], a code of honour and chivalry which stresses that martial arts are only to be employed when the safety of one's family, one's beloved or others are at stake and as a last resort. This is also one of the reasons why grappling or groundwork has not evolved much in China, as traditionally after falling one would allow one's opponent to get back up on their feet before continuing the combat.

⁴¹ Daoist Medicine is a rather modern term. See Michael Stanley-Baker, 'Daoing Medicine'.

⁴² A book on *fengshui* according to Li Shifu's teachings will be published in the future by Purple Cloud Press.

⁴³ There are two schools of *fengshui*, the Compass School and the Form School, both of which are deeply rooted in the phenomenon of qi. For instance, a bedroom in the wrong orientation, i.e. compass direction, can affect a person's health negatively according to the first school, while the second school argues that a house at the corner of a T-intersection, i.e. directly facing a busy and bustling road, creates disquietude and a stream of negative qi towards the house, with the same applying to sharp objects pointing at one's house, such as weaponry from statues to give an oft-cited example from premodern China.

⁴⁴ Li Shifu is here referring to the principles of treatment arising from a *Yi Jing* reading that overlap with *fengshui*. If a person or medicine is in the fire phase, for instance, then it would benefit that person to move to the south or work in the vicinity of fire, for example as a goldsmith or in a power station.

⁴⁵ 'Grasping hold of one's life' in Daoism signifies that one has gone beyond the influence of *yin* and *yang* and life and death.

⁴⁶ Li Shifu hints here at the notion that we can take no physical or non-physical attributes with us if we wish to enter higher realms or the Heavenly Kingdom.

⁴⁷ *Gong* can comprise any spiritual practice in this specific context, while in a general sense it refers to any form of skill.

⁴⁸ This passage is derived from the *Yi Jing*, 'Appended Remarks Part 1' (*xici shang* 系辞上). The full statement reads:

易無思也，無為也，寂然不動，感而遂通天下之故。

The *Yi* [signifies a state] without preoccupations and [interfering] actions. By being thereby quiet and unmoving and in resonance with this, one is able to communicate with the underlying causes [of all matters] under heaven.

This indicates that sensations and perceptions emerge from utter tranquillity. In the practice of deep stillness cultivation, therefore, movement is generated, including possibly the generation of *yang*, which ultimately leads to communion with higher realms.

49 Li Shifu uses the term 'seventh sense' to indicate that there are special abilities which go far beyond even the psychic intuition of a sixth sense.

50 Music in Daoism is held to be able to open the veil between the realm of form and the realm of the formless, as in many shamanic and religious traditions.

51 In Daoist tradition the incense carries prayers to the celestial realm. For that reason, there is an incense prayer to be recited when placing it in an incense bowl.

52 The Circular Temple Mound in Beijing is a good example of such a three-tier platform in ascending concentric circles. The platforms are the altar itself.

53 In Chinese, 誠 [*cheng*].

54 The 24th generation name of the Dragon Gate, to which both translators belong, is Sincerity [*cheng* 誠], which might be viewed as the Daoist lineage equivalent of a family name. The full Daoist name of Johan Hausen is Cheng Cai 誠材, literally 'Sincere Timber'.

55 Earth here denotes the netherworlds in opposition to the heavens, the upper realms.

56 External fields can be emanated by old trees, malign or benign entities, spirits and ghosts and so forth. To be sensitive enough to perceive them often requires rigorous training, yet some are born with an innate ability to sense them.

57 In Chinese, 用神 [*yongshen*], which is literally the 'applied spirit' or the 'employed spirit'. For a detailed discussion of this concept.

58 I.e. higher entities.

59 I.e. the lower elixir field [*dantian* 丹田], roughly located between the navel at the front and the kidneys at the back.

60 These are analogies for the monkey mind and one's racing thoughts.

61 Li Shifu is referring here to techniques for achieving stillness such as meditative practices.

62 For digging this grave-like cave in a nearby village named Nanshi, near Huxian 户县, Shaanxi Province, Wang Chongyang (1113–1170), the founder of the Complete Realization School, the most prominent Daoist school in China today, was dubbed the 'Living Dead'. Upon his re-emergence in 1163 he filled the pit with soil marking the end of his three-year cultivation period and moved to present-day Huxian, former Liujiang 劉蔣, in the Zhongnan Mountains, to live in a hut to continue his cultivation. After a further four years there he set it on fire while singing and dancing, with no sign of attachment to it. He died in 1170 and was buried in the Zhongnan Mountains. See also Johan Hausen and Allen Tsaur, chapter 24 in Book III, in *The 49 Barriers of Cultivating the Dao*, and Louis Komjathy, *The Way of Complete Perfection*, for more on Wang Chongyang.

63 Bodhidharma's final stage of cultivation mentioned here, in which he sat the facing the wall in his cave for nine years, has given its name to the Daoist process of 'Facing the Wall for Nine Years', the final, lengthy stage in the cultivation of the inner elixir, i.e. inner alchemy. Interestingly, this stage is not required for women since they are characterized by *yang* internally, unlike men who are *yin* on the inside, and thus women are closer to a state of complete *yang*, which signifies immortality.

64 Li Shifu implies that Jesus attained some of his powers through spiritual work in the so-called unknown years of Jesus that are not recorded in the gospels, from the ages of twelve to twenty-nine.

65 The full quote stems from *The Analects [of Confucius]*, chapter 16, 'Master Ji' (*jishi* 季氏):

孔子曰：生而知之者，上也；學而知之者，次也；困而學之，又其次也；困而不學，民斯為下矣。

Confucius said: 'Those who are born with knowledge are superior. Those who study and then become knowledgeable are next [in rank]. Those who are destitute and yet study are the next [in rank] … Those who are destitute and do not study are low [in rank].'

66 This statement is found in *The Analects [of Confucius]*, chapter 12, 'Yan Yuan' (顏淵).

67 This effect on one's karma will be either as the creation of a karmic attachment to controlling one's future or because one misses out on lessons in the cultivation of virtue (such as learning forbearance) by shunning any negative experiences.

68 This passage is from *The Scripture of the Hidden Talisman* (*Yinfu Jing* 陰符經). Note that in some versions 'lacking' (*qiong* 窮) is substituted by the homonym 躬 (*qiong*), denoting humility, with the sentence thus being 'they will become steady and humble'. For an English translation of the full text, see Louis Komjathy, 'Scripture of the Hidden Talisman'. 'To take lightly their life-destiny' is meant in a negative sense here, that these people squander their lives by not taking their life-destiny seriously.

69 These are not categories of virtues but rather denote that through moral conduct humans should model themselves on heaven, earth and the *dao*. In Daoism and Confucianism this is primarily achieved through the five basic ethical virtues and the precepts.

70 In Chinese thought, numbers tie in closely with mathematical astronomy and astrology. One's personal destiny, for example, has a number of breaths (*qi*) or a specific amount of *qi* allotted that determines the time of one's death. Similarly, in English we have the expression 'their hours are numbered' when someone is close to death. The Six Lines Method is entirely based on such a numerology, using the time when an oracle is cast to build the hexagram mathematically.

71 The three refuges, a concept borrowed from Buddhism – the tripartite Buddha, *dharma* and *sangha*, here means a reliance on one's physical body and one's lifetime at this given moment, which provide a unique opportunity for realization, and one's cognitive capacity, all of which are necessary for Daoist cultivation. For more on the three refuges of Daoism, see *The Dragon Gate's Core Methods* by Johan Hausen and Allen Tsaur (forthcoming).

72 Li Shifu does not reject this advanced method outright, but due to its hazardous nature, as one can develop cancer from it, he warns against using it. After shifting the cancer to oneself, this needs to be followed up by its expulsion from one's body. The method also has strict requirements with regard to one's mind and thinking and is not a technique that should be attempted by a novice.

73 Correctly executed, this method would entail that even though the cancer of the patient is imagined within oneself, it is subsequently purged so one does not end up with cancer oneself.

74 'In vain', with regard to the cancer example, refers not to the failure of the healing but to that of the healer's own cultivation by damaging the body and potentially destroying it, thus obstructing their practice and possibly removing the possibility of cultivation altogether.

[75] There is a distinction here between casting for money, fame, and professional or business ventures in contrast to casting for the sake of one' health. With the latter, it is crucial to cast an oracle in order to initiate healing and to eradicate disease, since this honours one's body as a unique vessel for cultivation.

[76] Even though you might seem to be losing on the material level, you are in fact eradicating bad karma through doing good.

[77] The Daoist notion of karma derived from one's ancestors indicates that one's karma is not only an individual affair from one's previous incarnations but is also inherited from one's family for three generations only. This principle of ancestral karma is affirmed in the following scriptures: Barbara Hendrischke, *The Scripture on Great Peace: The Taiping jng and the Beginnings of Daoism*, and Josh Paynter and Jack Schaefer, *The Northern Dipper Scripture: The Perfected Scripture of the Upmost Profoundly Numinous Northern Dipper That Prolongs Life and Affects Fundamental Destiny and Daoist Noon Altar Recitations: Sanguan Jing*.

[78] Since you are just the medium for the oracle, you carry no blame for what it reveals. See the story, 'Legends and Stories: The Solitary Neighbour'.

[79] In essence, a *Yi Jing* initiate harnesses the correspondences of the five phases to amend and alter a negative situation, either one at hand or predicted by the hexagram. They do so by strengthening or weakening certain phases through the eight compass directions, diet, clothing and the seasons, to name just a few of the means employed.

[80] In Chinese 煞法 (*shafa*). It is advised that such methods, which kill a negative entity through incantations, hand seals, and talismans, should only be used as an absolute last resort when all other techniques have failed, for instance negotiating and pleading with such a disease-causing entity to leave peacefully. This is based on one of the five cardinal precepts, 'do not kill', since killing any entity would go against this precept.

[81] See Johan Hausen and Allen Tsaur 'The Dragon Gate 100 Generation Poem' in *The Arts of Daoism*.

[82] *Gong* 功 denotes a special skill here.

[83] In Chinese, 隨口功 (*suikou gong*). *This skill is attained when an incantation can be recited as though the mouth were uttering the words by itself, without any conscious lead from the mind.*

84 I.e. the former abbess of Five Immortals Temple and Li Shifu's master. For more information on her life story and mission, see Johan Hausen and Allen Tsaur, appendix 9, 'Tao Fa Zhen' in *The Arts of Daoism*.

85 Louguan Tai is believed to be the place where Yin Xi 尹喜, the guardian of the pass, stopped Lao Zi and adamantly insisted that he transmit his teachings in writing, which resulted in the *Daode Jing*. For more on Yin Xi, see Johan Hausen and Allen Tsaur, chapter 3, 'Hibernating Dragon, II, 1.Yin Xi – The Gatekeeper' in *The Arts of Daoism*.

86 The Daoist Morning and Evening Scriptures are sung between 5–7am and 5–7pm respectively throughout all Complete Realization temples in China as part of the worship of the deities contained therein, and for the deliverance of all beings, alive and deceased alike. For a full translation, see Josh Paynter and Jack Schaefer, *Daoist Morning and Evening Altar Recitations*.

87 The recitation of scriptures, which includes specific declarations of deities of the Daoist pantheon, establishes a channel between the realm of humans and the celestial realm and in this way is able to grant otherworldly powers.

88 This most likely refers to the story of the Buddha and the murderer Angulimala, as recorded in the *Angulimala Sutta*.

89 The ten principal disciples vary according to the text consulted, however given the strong influence of Mahayana Buddhism on Daoism, it is safe to take the list of *Vimalakirti Nirdesa Sutra* here as authoritative. Li Shifu also alludes to an eleventh disciple here, the 'betrayer' of the Buddha, Devadatta, his cousin and brother-in-law, which points to his belief that a traitor offers the deepest lessons in the practice of forgiveness.

90 This notion can be observed in the higher two realms of the six realms of Buddhism, namely the realm of celestial beings (*devas*) and the realm of warlike demigods (*asuras*), and also in the novel *The Journey to the West*, allegedly written by Qiu Chuji, the founder of the Dragon Gate Sect.

91 See endnote 87.

92 The spirit lamp [*shendeng* 神燈] is an open oil lamp on the altar that is kept lit at all times of the day and night.

93 The extinguished spirit lamp and the fallen candle are both indicative of such negative energies.

[94] The foundations of sagehood are not laid in the jungle or in a cave, since seclusion comes at a much later stage and is useless without prior time in society to forge one's character and a peaceful mind.

[95] At the time of this talk, this was roughly the equivalent of 2500 US dollars.

[96] I.e. the nearest large city to the temple, which is approximately a two hours away from Five Immortals Temple.

[97] Li Shifu does not hold back in correcting his students' wrong thinking or actions, and openly tells them off when they have transgressed the precepts or done wrong.

[98] This requirement is stated in Liu Yiming, *The Script for Penetrating Through the Barriers* (*Tongguan Wen* 通关文), chapter 29:

三千功圓，八百果滿。

Three thousand [minor] merits [must be] accumulated, along with eight hundred [great] merits.

[99] See also Johan Hausen and Allen Tsaur, chapter 31, 'The Scripture of Clarity and Stillness' in Book III of *The 49 Barriers of Cultivating the Dao*.

[100] In summary, Li Shifu recommends that if the method of the *Yi Jing* is beyond one's comprehension, then one should just ask it a question with total sincerity in the hope that one will receive a message or inspiration from it in some form, and that this sincerity should also be expressed in one's moral conduct and way of life. Of course, it is extremely difficult to emulate the sages, who were in frequent contact with heaven, in their degree of sincerity. Nevertheless, if one does not have access to or does not understand the method of the *Yi Jing*, one should do one's best to act with sincerity in all circumstances, since ultimately this is beyond any method of the *Yi Jing*.

[101] The pebble refers to the three stones employed in creating the hexagram in a specific *Yi Jing* method.

[102] Li Shifu is aware that this notion may counteract humility at this stage and imbue the student with a sense of their own specialness so early on in their *Yi Jing* journey.

[103] In the narrow sense these two numbers are represented by the number of the heavenly stems, which cycle every ten days, and the number of the earthly branch, which cycles every twelve days. In the wider sense, the total number of the year, month, day and hour constitutes the lower trigram, representing earth, while the sum from year, month and day is said to correspond to the upper trigram, standing for heaven. It also

hints at heavenly and earthly phenomena such as weather changes and earthquakes or floods being predictable.

[104] A *chi* is a unit of measurement that represents one Chinese foot. Its exact length has changed through the dynasties, but it is roughly 1/3 metre. See also Johan Hausen and Allen Tsaur, chapter 17, 'The Spirit Illuminaries', in Book III of *The 49 Barriers of Cultivating the Dao*.

[105] The following passage from a Ming dynasty novel depicts a preparation of this kind in ancient China before the important activity of visiting a sage. According to chapter 24 of *The Naming List of the Investiture of the Spirits* (*Fengshen Bang* 封神榜), when the legendary King Wen sought to find the sage, Jiang Ziya, but was unable to do so, he returned to the palace to prepare for a second visit:

> 斋宿三日。至第四日，沐浴整衣，极其精诚，文王端坐鸾舆，扛抬聘礼。

> He fasted and remained in solitude for three days. On the fourth day, he washed and bathed, put on his [official] clothes and, with the greatest sincerity, King Wen sat upright in his imperial carriage [which then set off], [followed by his men who] carried on their shoulders the gifts [for the sage].

[106] Often translated as Temple of Heaven (*tiantan* 天壇). This is a complex of buildings dedicated to ceremonies that are directed to the heavens and is located in the southeast of central Beijing.

[107] This is often translated as 'Temple of Earth' (*ditan* 地壇). It is located directly opposite the Heavenly Altar in the northern part of central Beijing.

[108] Photograph by Felice Beato (1832–1909), 'Sacred Temple of Heaven Where the Emperor Sacrifices Once a Year in the Chinese City of Pekin' (October 1860).

[109] The following is an excerpt from *The Records of Rites* (*Liji* 禮記), written between the Warring States Period (5th century-221 BCE) and the Former Han Dynasty (206 BCE–8 CE), taken from the chapter 'Sacrificial Laws' (*jifa* 祭法):

> 燔柴於泰壇，祭天也 ；瘞埋於泰折，祭地也 ；用騂、犢。埋少牢於泰昭，祭時也 ；相近於坎、壇，祭寒暑也。

> Roasting sacrificial meat in firewood on the Platform of Peace is the sacrifice to heaven. Burying sacrifices in the Mound of Peace is the sacrifice to the earth; red horses and calves are used [as the sacrifices]. To bury [by making] sacrifices at the

> [Altar of the] Brightness of Peace is the sacrifice to the seasons, which is similar to the pit and altar [employed for] sacrifices to cold and heat.

The last sentence might either denote that the sacrifice happens at a fixed time, such as the summer and winter solstices, or that sacrifices were conducted to appease climatic conditions of extreme cold and heat. The practice of blood sacrifice continued until the end of the Qing Dynasty. See Terry Kleeman, 'Licentious Cults and Bloody Victuals: Sacrifice, Reciprocity, and Violence in Traditional China'.

[110] Moxibustion is a medical treatment in which the practitioner burns the herb mugwort (*Artemisia arghi/vulgaris*) to heat up certain body parts or specific acupuncture points.

[111] For instance, in buildings with fire alarms, in unventilated areas, or when people have any kind of compromised respiratory functioning, not to speak of the inconvenience of having to carry incense on one's body or in one's car at all times.

[112] The images below may help to clarify the finger positions:

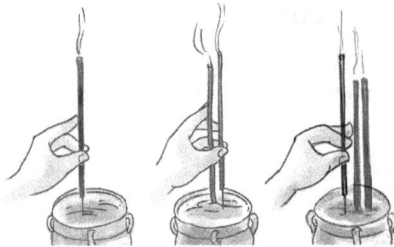

[113] Insert person's name.

[114] There seems to have been a substantial crossover between this incantation and the first divination lot of *Zhuge Liang's Spirit Calculations* (*Zhuge Shensuan* 諸葛神算):

> 伏羲神農文王周公孔子，五代聖人及鬼谷先生，占卦童子，翻卦童郎，空中一切過往神祇：今弟子某省（市）、某縣、某鄉、某某（姓名），某年某月，今因為某事，憂疑未決，謹自虔心誠意，於三十二課內佔一課，吉凶禍福，成敗興亡，報應分明，急急如律令。

> [This disciple calls on] Fu Xi, the Divine Farmer, King Wen, the Duke of Zhou, Confucius, the sages of the five dynasties (the Yellow Emperor, King Yao, King Shun, King Yu the

Great, and King Tang of Shang) and the teacher Guigu [Zi] [lit. Master Ghost Valley], the Hexagram-Casting Infant Boy and the Hexagram-Everting Infant youth, and all spirits and earth deities in the empty space of the past. At the present moment, this disciple from a certain province (city), a certain county, a certain town, and of a certain (family name and first name), [born in] a certain year and a certain month, because of a certain matter at this present moment, [this disciple] is worried, doubtful and hesitant to make a decision. Solemnly, with a reverential heart-mind and sincere intent, [this disciple] wishes to receive a divination slip from among the thirty-two slips, [to see] whether [the matter at hand] will be auspicious or inauspicious, and [whether it will bring] fortune or misfortune, success or failure, flourishing or decay, and to make clear the repercussions [of the situation]. [May this request be received] quickly and swiftly in accordance with the statutes and ordinances!

[115] *Si* is pronounced *ci* in Standard Mandarin.

[116] These are assistants and helpers, just like the smaller statues in a main temple at either side of the main deities, or like the servants of an emperor.

[117] The Original Honoured One, *ishtadevata* in Sanskrit, is a tutelary deity or a meditation deity of personal nature, a term from Hinduism depicting the devotee's favourite deity.

[118] Insert your name and the subject matter of the oracle you are casting, for instance in a concise and succinct way such as 'Cheng Jiu – practising *gong*' [*chéngjiǔ liàngōng* 誠久煉功], or 'Cheng Cai – going on a journey [*chéng cái chūxíng* 誠才出行].

[119] This incantation can be adjusted depending on whether one casts a trigram or a hexagram; the latter is signposted in brackets and to be replaced in the Chinese, when reciting.

[120] The hexagram descends from the higher realms.

[121] If a hexagram, instead of a trigram, is cast, then '*bāchúnguà*' is replaced by '*bābāliùshísìguà*' in the parenthesis.

[122] The brackets are for when this incantation is used for casting a hexagram. See endnote 120.

[123] This refers to the shaking of three coins within the hollow of one's clasped hands, which is part of the coin tossing method.

124 I.e. materials such as pen, paper, and the casting devices such as yarrow sticks, coins or bamboo horns.

125 This story is also found in an abbreviated form in Lindsey Wei, *The Valley Spirit: A Story of Daoist Cultivation*.

126 This is in line with the method that utilizes the trigrams rather than the hexagrams and the latter's statements [*guaci* 卦辭].

127 I.e. 7–11am.

128 For the two other stories on this topic, see below ('Solitary Neighbour' and 'Family Feud').

129 In Chinese 仙境 (*xianjing*).

130 The couple suspected that their cousin had been tempted by the opportunity to sell their cow to the butcher.

131 I.e. Li Shifu.

132 Li Shifu does not charge a fixed rate; instead, he accepts gifts or asks the recipient to give a donation in the main temple hall to express their gratitude.

133 See chapter 1, 'The Yi Jing Virtues and Karma', endnote 69.

134 In Chinese, 屋山 (*wushan*). This seems to be the part of the roof above the gable which is also called 'mountain wall' Chinese, 山牆 (*shanqiang*).

135 I.e. San Francisco; in Chinese, 旧金山 (*jiujinshan*).

136 In Chinese the complete name is '*Yi [Jing]* Numerology Apricot Method' (*meihua yishu* 梅花易數). This method is commonly known as the 'Plum Blossom Method', but this has been demonstrated to be a misnomer by Eugene Anderson in personal communication. The fruit in question, in Latin the *Prunus mume*, the sour apricot or East Asian apricot, looks strikingly different from a 'plum'. See Lorraine Wilcox, 'Plum Flower Divination and Medicine', and Da Liu, *I Ching Numerology: Based on Shao Yung's Classic Plum Blossom Numerology* for a practical account of this method.

137 Culturally it may have been considered inappropriate to make visits around dinner time.

138 This refers to the five phases – wood, fire, earth, metal and water – that correspond to the two trigrams that were cast. So the upper trigram was either *qian* or *dui* and the lower trigram either *zhen* or *xun*, hence 'metal' and 'wood'. A hexagram is read by its upper trigram first, followed by its lower trigram.

[139] I.e. divination is never clear-cut, as a sign or omen can easily be mis-interpreted. Of course, there are dozens of items made of wood and metal, and therefore the wife and husband both read the oracle differently here.

[140] Celestial time stands in the widest sense for the 'right timing' but can refer more specifically to the appropriate season that favours an undertaking.

[141] On another occasion, Li Shifu alluded to this story in the following way: 'If a neighbour knocked on your door at night and you then quickly cast a hexagram of wood above, metal below, this would generally indicate something like a hoe or shovel or axe, since its handle is made of wood and its blade of metal. However, how could he possibly be asking for a hoe or shovel at that time unless he wanted to dig up a grave, since tomb raiding only happens at night? You must reconsider your interpretation according to what is the most likely scenario at that given time of the day. Even if he were to ask for an axe, who chops wood at night? So abide by the common practices of life. Interpret the omens that appear in your reading according to the things that ninety-nine per cent of all people do at certain times, such as sleeping at night and eating in the morning, rather than on the anomalies of the one per cent.'

[142] I.e. in rural communities, chores must not be left till the last minute, or the consequences might be dire. Thus, the collecting and cutting of wood is taken care off well before there is a shortage and in weather conditions that are not hostile, such as a sunny and mild day and not in deep snow or during rain or hail.

[143] The crux of the story is that in one's reading it is wisest to follow the majority of people in their traditions and habits, i.e. most people sleep at night. This is what is meant by the heavenly, earthly and human principle. Anyone or any action going against such principles is incredibly hard to predict, but luckily will always be a rare exception.

[144] This is Li Shifu's retelling of a story from *The Romance of the Three Kingdoms*, chapter 46, 'Employing an Extraordinary Strategy Kong Ming Borrows Arrows, Putting on Display a Secret Plan Huang Gai Is Executed' (*yong qimou kong ming jiejian, xian miji huanggai shouxing* 用奇謀孔明借箭，獻密計黃蓋受刑). For a complete translation, see Moss Roberts, *Three Kingdoms*.

[145] This illustration is from *Romance of the Three Kingdoms in Illustrations* (*Sanguozhi Tuxiang* 三國志圖像), 'artist unknown'. The preface written in 164 by Jin Renrui 金人瑞, later changed to Jin Shengtan 金聖歎,

literally 'Sage Sigh', (1608–1661), a late Ming and early Qing literary critic, may help tentatively to date this text. For more on Jin Shengtan see Ding Nafei, 'The Manic Preface: Jin Shengtan's (1608–1661) Shuihu Zhuan', and Sally K. Church, 'Beyond the Words: Jin Shengtan's Perception of Hidden Meanings in Xixiang Ji', and Ge Liangyan, 'Authoring "Authorial Intention:" Jin Shengtan as Creative Critic'.

[146] The story has been adapted into a scene in the popular film *Red Cliff* (*Chibi* 赤壁), a famous Chinese blockbuster that was internationally released 2008–2009. For more on Zhuge Liang see also Stefan Kappstein, *Zhuge Liang: Shen Shu – Das Orakel der Heiligen Zahlen*, He Yujing and Justin McNulty, *The Magical Lots of ZhuGe Liang: Divination Using the I Ching* and Ralph Sawyer, *Zhuge Liang: Strategy, Achievements and Writings*.

[147] This story not only exemplifies the power of mantic practices and their applicability, but also the ingenuity of the mastermind Zhuge Liang, one of the most famous diviners in Chinese history.

[148] The story can also be found in a slightly different form in *The Journey to the West*, chapter 10, translated by William Jenner.

[149] This shows a scene from *The Journey to the West with Illustrations* (*Huiben Xiyou Ji* 西遊記), drawn by Toya Ohara 大原東野 (1771–1840), from Chapter 9, 'Yuan Shoucheng's Foresight Without Selfish Bias – The Old Dragon King's Clumsy Ruse Violates the *Heavenly Edict*' (*yuan shoucheng miaosuan wusi qu lao longwang zhuoji fan tiantiao* 袁守誠妙算無私曲 老龍王拙計犯天條). This work also contains drawings by Utagawa Toyohiro 歌川豐廣 (1773–1828) and Katsushika Taito II 葛飾戴斗 (fl. 1810–1853).

[150] Yuan Tian Gang 袁天罡 (573–645) was the president of the Imperial Board of Astronomy (*Chao Qintianjian Taizheng* 朝欽天監台正).

[151] Surprisingly, to this day the Chinese government has yet to approve excavations on the site. Debates are ongoing about whether China has the necessary technical equipment for a safe excavation and for the protection of the unearthed treasures within the tomb.

[152] The Dragon King is the Chinese deity in charge of water and weather and is still revered in many coastal regions. For more on this deity, see Daniel Overmyer, Local Religion in North China in the Twentieth Century the Structure and Organization of Community Rituals and Beliefs, and Andreas Berndt, 'Der Kult der Drachenkönige (longwang) im China der späten Kaiserzeit'.

[153] As the ruler over bodies of water, all water creatures are considered to be his family members.

¹⁵⁴ The moral implication here is that it is wrong to take life out of greed (or for pleasure, like hunting) by calculating oracles.

¹⁵⁵ I.e. the weather.

¹⁵⁶ The Jade Emperor is often considered to be at the very pinnacle of the Daoist pantheon. His praises are chanted as the centrepiece of the *Daoist Morning Scripture*. See Josh Paynter and Jack Schaefer, *The Daoist Morning and Evening Altar Recitations*.

¹⁵⁷ There are many levels of command in the celestial order, just as there are in a government, which is why the Dragon King is able to sabotage Yuan Shoucheng's prediction by not following the orders of his superior.

¹⁵⁸ Naturally Yuan Shoucheng was suspicious since his predictions were always utterly accurate and so he was aware that a higher force must have been at play.

¹⁵⁹ Although the Dragon King is a deity, he is represented here, with the creative licence of a novel, as a mortal whose life can be ended.

¹⁶⁰ It is heavily implied that the old lady sought out Li Shifu for a ceremony or ritual that directly affects one's karma and life trajectory by pleading, praying and making offerings to the deities of the Daoist pantheon in order to be granted a longer lifespan.

¹⁶¹ This is stressed here as an actual event since some of the other stories come from novels. A westerner may be more critical or doubtful, suspecting that she would have outlived the predictions anyway, but for the Chinese such predictions are to be taken much more seriously and the daughter would have been entirely distraught upon hearing such dire news.

Bibliography

Adler, J. (2020) *The Original Meaning of the Yijing: Commentary on the Scripture of Change.* New York: Columbia University Press

Berkowitz , A. and Cook, D. (1703) Letter J18 May 1703 Leibniz to Bouvet', Retrieved 1st June 2022 from: https://leibniz-bouvet. swarthmore.edu/letters/letter-j-18-may-1703-leibniz-to-bouvet

Berndt, A. (1982) Der Kult der Drachenkönige (longwang) im China der späten Kaiserzeit, (Ph.D. Diss.) Universität Leipzig

Church, S. K. (1999) 'Beyond the words: Jin Shengtan's

Perception of Hidden Meanings in Xixiang ji', *Harvard Journal of Asiatic Studies 59*: 5–77

Drasny, J. (2018) The Regular Grouping of the Hexagrams before the Yi jing - The King Wen Groups. Retrieved 3 February 2023 from: http://www.i-ching.hu/array/kingwen-groups-z.pdf

Felley, G. (2013) Yintelligence: The Mapping of the Pre-Heaven or FuXi Hexagrams to the Post-Heaven or King Wen Hexagrams. *Chinese Studies 2* (4): 197–203. DOI:10.4236/chnstd.2013.24032

Flieder, K. (2007) 'The Yijing – The Philosophical Foundation of the Binary System?', in László Böszörmenyi (ed.), *MEDICHI 2007 – Methodic and Didactic Challenges of the History of Informatics.* Klagenfurt, Austria: Österreichische Computer Gesellschaft

Ge, L. (2003) Authoring 'Authorial Intention': Jin Shengtan as Creative Critic', *Chinese Literature: Essays, Articles, Reviews 25*: 1–24

Hausen, J. and Tsaur, A. (2020) *The 49 Barriers of Cultivating the Dao.* Auckland: Purple Cloud Press

—. (2021) *The Arts of Daoism.* Auckland: Purple Cloud Press

—. (forthcoming 2024) *The Dragon Gate's Core Methods.* Auckland: Purple Cloud Press

He. Y. and McNulty, J. (2011) The Magical Lots of ZhuGe Liang: Divination Using the I Ching. No place: CreateSpace Independent Publishing

Hendrischke, B. (2015) *The Scripture on Great Peace: The Taiping Jing and the Beginnings of Daoism*. Berkeley: University of California Press

Jenner, W. (2014) *Journey to the West*. Beijing: Foreign Language Press

Kappstein, S. (1996) *Zhuge Liang: Shen Shu – Das Orakel der Heiligen Zahlen*. Seeshaupt & München: Ryvellus Medienverlag

Kleeman, T. (1994) Licentious Cults and Bloody Victuals: Sacrifice, Reciprocity, and Violence in Traditional China. *Asia Major* 7 (1): 185–211 DOI:10.2307/41645504

Komjathy, L. (2013) *The Way of Complete Perfection: A Quanzhen Daoist Anthology*. Albany: State University of New York Press

Liu, D. (1979) *I Ching Numerology: Based on Shao Yung's Classic Plum Blossom Numerology*. San Francisco: Harper & Row

Lodder, J. (2009) Binary Arithmetic: From Leibniz to von Neumann. In Brian Hopkins (ed.), *Resources for Teaching Discrete Mathematics: Classroom Projects, History Modules, and Articles*. Washington, D.C.: Mathematical Association of America

Marshall, S. (2001) *The Mandate of Heaven: Hidden History in the I Ching*. New York: Columbia University Press

Overmyer, D. (2009) *Local Religion in North China in the Twentieth Century the Structure and Organization of Community Rituals and Beliefs*. Brill: Leiden

Paynter, J. and Schaefer, J. (2019) *Daoist Morning and Evening Altar Recitations*. New York and Colorado: Parting Clouds Press

—. (2020) *Daoist Noon Altar Recitations: Sanguan Jing*. New York and Colorado: Parting Clouds Press

—. (2021) *The Northern Dipper Scripture: The Perfected Scripture of the Upmost Profoundly Numinous Northern Dipper That Prolongs Life and Affects Fundamental Destiny*. New York and Colorado: Parting Clouds Press

Roberts, M. (1995) *Three Kingdoms*. Beijing: Foreign Languages Press

Ryan, J. (1996) Leibniz' Binary System and Shao Yong's "Yijing', *Philosophy East and West*, 46(1): 59–90

Shaughnessy, E. (2014) *Unearthing the Changes: Recently Discovered Manuscripts of the Yi Jing (I Ching) and Related Texts*. New York: New York Columbia Press

Stanley-Baker, M. (2019) Daoing Medicine, *East Asian Science, Technology, and Medicine* 50: 21–66

Sun, Y. (2019) The Interpretation of Hetu and Luoshu, *Linguistics and Literature Studies* 8(4):190–194 DOI:10.13189/lls.2020.080404

Swetz, F. (2003) Leibniz, the Yijing, and the religious Conversion of the Chinese, *Mathematics Magazine* 76(4): 276–291

Wei, L. (2010) *The Valley Spirit: A Story of Daoist Cultivation*. London: Line of Intent

Wilcox, L. (2006) Plum Flower Divination and Medicine. Retrieved 24 July 2022 from:https://www.academia.edu/28252329/Plum_Flower_Divination_and_Medicine